Considering Veritatis Splendor

Considering
VERITATIS
SPLENDOR

Edited by John Wilkins

The Pilgrim Press
Cleveland, Ohio

Originally published by the Society for Promoting Christian
Knowledge, London, as *Understanding Veritatis Splendor*, © 1994
by Society for Promoting Christian Knowledge

Pilgrim Press edition published 1994
The Pilgrim Press, Cleveland, Ohio 44115

Printed in Great Britain

99 98 97 96 95 94 5 4 3 2 1

ISBN 0-8298-1007-2

Contents

The Contributors

John Wilkins is the Editor of *The Tablet*

Lisa Sowle Cahill is Professor of Theology at Boston College and a past president of the Catholic Theological Society of America.

John Finnis is Professor of Law and Legal Philosophy in the University of Oxford.

Josef Fuchs SJ is Professor Emeritus of Moral Theology at the Gregorian University, Rome, where he taught from 1954 to 1992.

Germain Grisez is the Flynn Professor of Christian Ethics at Mount St Mary's College, Maryland.

Bernhard Häring CSSR is Professor Emeritus of the Alphonsianum, Rome, and the author of some eighty books, including the multi-volume series, *The Law of Christ*, and *Free and Faithful in Christ*.

Nicholas Lash is the Norris-Hulse Professor of Divinity at the University of Cambridge.

Herbert McCabe OP teaches theology at the University of Oxford.

Richard McCormick SJ is the John A. O'Brien Professor of Christian Ethics at the University of Notre Dame, Indiana.

Oliver O'Donovan is Regius Professor of Moral and Pastoral Theology at Oxford University

Mary Tuck is a criminologist and social scientist, and former head of research in the Home Office, London.

Maciej Zieba OP lectures at the Pontifical Academy of Theology in Krakow and at the University of Poznan.

Introduction

John Wilkins

In Western culture today there is a widespread moral unease. People feel that something is wrong. The task of establishing a pluralist society which yet acknowledges shared values as the condition of that pluralism is proving beyond the capacities at present being brought to it. There is a loss of the link between freedom and truth—the truth that sets you free.

Into that situation Pope John Paul II released his encyclical letter *Veritatis Splendor* on 6 August 1993. Few papal documents of modern times have been awaited with such anticipation. Public opinion had been excited by a leaked draft in which the Church's infallibility was applied to the exposition of the natural law. A number of theologians expressed deep alarm. That particular passage, however, was not included in the encyclical when it finally appeared. The history of the text will one day be visible and will throw light on the debates that went into its production and the winners and losers in that process.

Veritatis Splendor is addressed to all the bishops of the Catholic Church but makes appeal to all people of good will, and secular opinion was ready to admit the accurate aim of the shafts it launched against the relativism of the age. It is informed throughout by a sense of burning urgency. The Pope sees a crisis in the world which is reflected in the Church. Having watched one hostile ideology—Communist collectivism—collapse during his papacy, he now rides out against another—the ethical relativism of liberal society.

Everyone knows the malady he refers to. An instance of it was described last year by a Jesuit writing in a publication of the American Catholic bishops. A class was invited to consider a typical moral dilemma that might be faced by a young woman. This was the dialogue that ensued:

Teacher: "So those are the choices open to her. What should she do?"

Students: "It's up to her."

Teacher: "Yes, I know it's up to her. But what should she do?"

Students: "It's her choice."

Teacher: "Yes, we know it's her choice. But how should she choose? And on what grounds?"

Students: "It's her choice."

The exchange illustrates precisely the assumptions against which *Veritatis Splendor* directs its fire: the absence of any sense of an objective moral order; the assertion of freedom over truth; conscience understood as the arbiter of the moral law instead of its vehicle.

Veritatis Splendor falls into three sections. The first is an extended meditation on the story in Matthew's gospel of the rich young man who came to Jesus asking what he had to do to be perfect, and who went away in sorrow when told that he should give his possessions to the poor. The Pope's interpretation presents the challenge of the parable with great power, expounding the wisdom of the text in meditative fashion rather than providing an exegesis of it. The cost of this approach is to spiritualise the hard message of this story in a way the liberation theologians would be likely to question.

The second section contains the core of the argument, in a quite different style which suggests that other hands have been at work. Here the encyclical sets out to show that it is possible to define certain acts as wrong in themselves, independently of intention or consequences, so that they are forbidden in all circumstances, and it criticises the schools which evaluate the moral task according to other perspectives. It rests its thesis on the twin basis of biblical revelation (the ten commandments) and the natural law which though of divine origin is in principle accessible to everyone. This second section also contains a treatment of conscience which is of central importance. The essential point being made is that it is the task of conscience to discover and act on truths which are already present, not to create values and duties of its own.

The final section includes a hymn to martyrdom as the epitome of an ethics founded on non-utilitarian principles. The martyrs point beyond neo-Darwinism.

The articles in this book, reprinted from the Catholic weekly *The Tablet* which I edit, vary in their appraisal. All share the encyclical's concern for the connection between truth and freedom. All agree that truth is antecedent and can be known and that it entails a consequent way of life. All think that moral obligations are discovered, not invented. So all welcome the Pope's recall to first principles. But while they accept that they are obliged by doctrine authoritatively taught, the supporting arguments which are used do not bind them; and here the opinion of these contributors diverges.

The crucial question is how far certain acts can indeed be defined always and everywhere as wrong, independently of intentions and consequences. It is significant that the encyclical reads the sixth commandment as "You shall not murder", not "You shall not kill." For as Professor Häring points out in his chapter, the Christian tradition has not held that the prohibition of killing applies to self-defence, or participation in a just war, or exaction of the death penalty. Professor Finnis further elaborates the definition as "Never choose to kill an innocent human being". Yet even so the question can arise, who exactly are to be defined as the innocent?

In any event the encyclical should not be taken as playing down the importance of intention and consequences in moral evaluation. It could hardly do so in view of Christian tradition. St Augustine, for example, to whom the encyclical appeals, was insistent on intention as the crux in moral judgment. Otherwise the guiding principle for him is the golden rule—"do to others as you would wish them to do to you"—valid for everyone in every place and at every time.

St Augustine and St Thomas were well aware that duties can conflict. So if her child is dying of hunger, a woman can steal food for it. For the right to private property is not absolute and it gives way to "the universal destination of all the world's goods", to quote the words of Vatican II.

St Augustine gives another example. In his commentary on the sermon on the mount, he tells the story of a woman whose husband was in prison for debt, owing a pound of gold which he could not pay. After consulting him, the woman agreed to sleep for one night with a rich man who desired her and who offered to provide the gold in return. Augustine refuses to censure her for what she did. "I offer no opinion either way about this story", he observes. "Let each person form a judgment as he pleases."

Before the encyclical was published, secular opinion was sure that it would be all about sex. It is not. But certainly its analysis of moral acts is particularly fitted to personal life, rather than to political or social engagement, as Professor Lash argues: and clearly contraception is envisaged as one of those acts which are always and everywhere forbidden irrespective of intention and consequences. Here we come to the "meaning of this document for the family quarrel" to which Professor O'Donovan refers, for it has been sexual ethics which in recent decades have caused most disagreement within the Catholic family. Though contraception is hardly mentioned in *Veritatis Splendor*, what it does say is enough. As Professor Lisa Cahill observes, traditional sexual norms can be given more or less emphasis as the essential reference of the encyclical, according to the wishes of the particular commentator. On any account, the Pope would appear to have made the possibility of a future modification of the Church's ban on contraception still harder.

It is a ban which has not been accepted by a very large number of Catholics. They make the Church's pro-life perspectives their own, but they do not regard contraception as intrinsically wrong. They observe, for example, that in Paul VI's encyclical *Humanae Vitae* it is stated that contraception is admissible for therapeutic purposes. So intention counts. All these therefore are "dissenters", in the terminology of this encyclical. Some contributors to this book appear ready to see the weaker brethren depart, but it is unlikely they will do so. Precisely because of this teaching on contraception which they cannot accept, they have profoundly modified their understanding of the relationship between authority and the informed conscience of the individual.

What is the role of these others in the reception of the encyclical? Do they have a part to play, or are they simply to be passive? Is that what "reception" really means? The encyclical thinks so. It is wholly structured, in Bernhard Häring's view, towards enforcing absolute obedience to every utterance of the Pope. The cry of distress which Häring, probably the best known of Catholic moral theologians, utters in his article should give pause to everyone.

The role of conscience is crucial. Men and women in the United States and Britain inherit a particularly strong sense of the authority of conscience, and the Roman Catholic Church will not succeed in appealing to their deepest convictions unless it is seen to do full justice to that voice which Newman called, in an exceptionally daring phrase, "the first of the Vicars of Christ"—another way of saying, as he also did, that "I will drink to the Pope by all means, but to conscience first".

Veritatis Splendor powerfully rebuts the false view of conscience everywhere current which is epitomised in the discussion between teachers and students recounted above. But is there a risk that it dethrones the informed conscience in relation to authority? So long as conscience means resisting totalitarianism, there is nothing but applause for it from the Pope. But as soon as conscience starts operating in the personal ethical sphere, his cautions mount. The encyclical stresses that conscience is subject to error, needs shaping, has to work hard, requires help from the tradition and insights of the community. Yet there is no reflection of this essential dialogue in the encyclical itself.

In keeping with its rigorism, *Veritatis Splendor* urges its readers to be ready to accept spiritual martyrdom as the epitome of the moral life. Such an aspiration for the Church is characteristic of Pope John Paul II's leadership. But it is not obvious that most martyrdoms do in fact come about as testimonies to ethics, rather than to faith. Moreover, here a gap might seem to threaten to open up between teaching and the pastoral situation. The greatest sorrow is not to be a saint, but most people are sinners, and in the case of sinners God has to write straight with crooked lines, which means so often that the moral task is to proceed from one inadequate situation to another in a good direction. And it should always be as pastors that bishops do the kinds of teaching they are called to do.

The Pope is definite that other approaches are not ruled out. "Certainly", he says, the teaching authority of the Church "does not intend to impose upon the faithful any particular theological system, still less a philosophical one". Some of the contributors to this volume who represent those other schools—Fr Fuchs and Fr McCormick, for example, both of whom feel that the encyclical has not done justice to their position—will want to emphasise that papal assurance. Without it, this encyclical will be bad news for Christian moral theologians belonging to these other schools. All of them desire to develop a dialogue with moral philosophers in the secular world, which cannot be done if the starting-point has to be that the only true foundation for ethics is the one elaborated in *Veritatis Splendor*.

"It is a great encyclical", a well-known Catholic professor of philosophy said to me. "When I read it, I am sometimes frightened by its power in the same way as when I read the gospels." Will that opinion be widely shared? In the light of history, will *Veritatis Splendor* be seen merely as another plank in a policy of restoration that was doomed to fail? Or will it, instead, be regarded as a landmark in a retreat from relativism where the Christian Church was able to play a part in toppling this other demon? Or will it, less dramatically than either but more usefully, serve as an aid to clarifying some of the deepest confusions of our time? Somewhere between the crashed collectivism of Communism and the inadequacies of liberal individualism lies a better way. That is what *Veritatis Splendor* is about.

Revelation versus dissent

Germain Grisez

The descriptive title of Pope John Paul II's new encyclical, *Veritatis Splendor*, indicates its subject matter: "De fundamentis doctrinae moralis Ecclesiae (On the foundations of the Church's moral teaching)". And speaking directly to the bishops, to whom the document as a whole is addressed, the Pope is more specific: "Each of us knows how important is the teaching which represents the central theme of this encyclical and which is today being restated with the authority of the Successor of Peter." That central theme, he continues, is: "the reaffirmation of the universality and immutability of the moral commandments, particularly those which prohibit always and without exception intrinsically evil acts" (115).

The Pope addresses his brother bishops, he says, "in obedience to the word of the Lord who entrusted to Peter the task of strengthening his brethren" (115). The Pope and the bishops are "facing what is certainly a genuine crisis" (5). For "a new situation has come about within the Christian community itself . . . It is no longer a matter of limited and occasional dissent, but of an overall and systematic calling into question of traditional moral doctrine" (4).

The encyclical does not deal with specific kinds of acts, such as contraception or abortion, homosexual behaviour or adultery. Rather, it examines and finds wanting dissenting views that attempt to find a way around some or all of the precepts which exclude those or other acts as always wrong.

As the foundation for his criticism of such dissent, the Pope recalls that faith includes specific moral requirements. The encyclical's whole first chapter unfolds the significance of Jesus' dialogue with the rich young man described in chapter 19 of Matthew's gospel. Here the Pope finds Jesus reaffirming as God's word some specific requirements which everyone must meet if he or she is to be saved.

These requirements are not arbitrary: "The commandments of which Jesus reminds the young man are meant to safeguard the good of the person, the image of God, by protecting his· goods. 'You shall not murder; You shall not commit adultery'" and so on, formulated as prohibitions, "express with particular force the ever urgent need to protect human life, the communion of persons in marriage" (13), and so on. Moreover, "Jesus shows that the commandments are not to be understood as a minimum limit not to be gone beyond, but rather as a path involving a moral and spiritual journey toward perfection, at the heart of which is love" (15). While perfection is far more, "one can 'abide' in love only be keeping the commandments" (24).

The encyclical points out that God has communicated the same moral requirements both as natural law, by giving human persons understanding of what is right and wrong, and as revealed truth. Since grace perfects human nature, Christian morality, while going beyond natural law, always includes it. "From the very lips of Jesus, the new Moses, man is once again given the commandments of the Decalogue" (12). Indeed, Jesus' "way of acting and his words, his deeds and his precepts constitute the moral rule of Christian life" (20). That is why the requirements of natural law are included in the Gospel, so that "the Gospel is 'the source of all saving truth and moral teaching'" (28).

While the encyclical's first chapter provides an inspiring articulation of the Gospel's teaching about following Jesus, its second chapter takes up and criticises four ways in which various dissenters have tried to soften received moral teaching about intrinsically evil acts.

One way is to affirm that Christians must love their neighbour and respect everyone's dignity but to deny that love and respect always forbid "intrinsically evil acts"—such as killing the innocent and adultery. Of course, proponents of this view can say that murder and adultery are wrong provided "murder" means unjust killing and "adultery" means unchaste or irresponsible intercourse involving someone married to a third party. But until some moralists began looking for ways around the precepts forbidding intrinsically evil acts, no Jew or Christian ever gave the fifth and sixth commandments so vacuous an interpretation. A more substantive defence of this view asserts that specific prohibitions result from "biologism" or "naturalism" (47), i.e., from confusing what is naturally given with what morally ought to be.

In replying, the Pope recalls the Church's definitive teaching on the human person's unity and argues: since the human person "entails a particular spiritual and bodily structure, the primordial moral requirement of loving and respecting the person as an end and never as a mere means also implies, by its very nature, respect for certain fundamental goods" (48), such as bodily life and marital communion.

Ultimately, however, attempts to limit Christian morality's requirements to generalities such as love and respect are rejected by the Pope on the ground that they are "contrary to the teaching of Scripture and Tradition" (49). He quotes St Paul's condemnation (in 1 Cor. 6.9–10) of "certain specific kinds of behaviour the wilful acceptance of which prevents believers from sharing in the inheritance promised to them"(49), and recalls Trent's use of the same passage against a view somewhat like the one rejected here.

A second way around the precepts forbidding intrinsically evil acts is to treat them as sound guidelines, but mere guidelines, for conscience. On this view, only conscience can decide whether an act bad in general might be appropriate in a concrete situation.

The Pope's reply is that this view mistakenly treats conscience as a creative decision rather than as a judgment following from moral truths, including negative precepts which oblige in every case (see 56). Once more, the Pope appeals to St Paul, this time to Rom. 2:15, which "clarifies the precise nature of conscience: it is a moral judgment about man and his actions, a judgment either of acquittal or of condemnation, according as human acts are in conformity or not with the law of God written on the heart" (59).

Certain theories of fundamental option provide a third way of softening the impact of precepts excluding intrinsically evil acts. Though such acts may be intrinsically wrong, doing them in particular cases, even with full awareness and deliberate consent, need not reverse one's option for the good and for God, and so need not be mortal sin.

The Pope rejects such theories as inconsistent with the make-up of the acting person. But even before doing so, he rejects them as "contrary to the teaching of Scripture itself, which sees the fundamental option as a genuine choice of freedom and links that choice profoundly to particular acts" (67). The "choice of freedom" which "Christian moral teaching, even in its biblical roots, acknowledges" as fundamental is "the decision of faith . . . the obedience of faith (cf. Rom. 16:26)" by which (again quoting Vatican II's constitution on divine revelation) "man makes a total and free self-commitment to God, offering 'the full submission of intellect and will to God as he reveals'" (66). Since faith is a commitment to covenantal communion with God, which is to bear fruit in works, it entails the specific requirements of the Decalogue, reaffirmed by Jesus as conditions for entering the Kingdom.

The fourth and final way by which many dissenting moralists circumvent traditional teaching is by flatly denying that the precepts forbidding certain kinds of acts as intrinsically evil really are exceptionless. Proportionalists or consequentialists maintain that one cannot always tell that an act excluded by such a precept would be morally evil without taking into account, in the actual circumstances, the greater good or lesser evil which it might bring about. They maintain that the foreseen proportions of "pre-moral" or "ontic" goods to bads in the available alternatives can require an exception even to such precepts as the fifth and sixth commandments, as traditionally understood.

Against these theories, the Pope points out "the difficulty, or rather the impossibility, of evaluating all the good and evil consequences and effects—defined as pre-moral—of one's own acts" (77). He goes on to argue that the morality of human acts depends on their "object", which, being "a freely chosen kind of behaviour" . . . is "the proximate end of a deliberate decision which determines the act of willing on the part of the acting person" (78). But the objects of certain kinds of acts are at odds with "the goods safeguarded by the commandments" (79). Thus: "Reason attests that there are objects of the human act which are by their nature 'incapable of being ordered' to God, because they radically contradict the good of the person made in his image. These are the acts which, in the Church's moral tradition, have been termed 'intrinsically evil' (*intrinsece malum*): they are such always and *per se*, in other words, on account of their very object, and quite apart from the ulterior intentions of the one acting and the circumstances" (80).

But, once again, the Pope's critique finally invokes revelation: "In teaching the existence of intrinsically evil acts, the Church accepts the teaching of Sacred Scripture" (81). Two texts are cited, Rom. 3:8 and (once more) I Cor. 6:9–10. The former first appears in a quotation from St Thomas (in 78), then in the heading to sections 79–83, and finally in a quotation from *Humanae Vitae* 14, where Paul VI taught that "it is never lawful, even for the gravest reasons, to do evil that good may come of it (cf. Rom. 3:8)" (80). Finally, John Paul also teaches: "The doctrine of the object as a source of morality represents an authentic explicitation of the biblical morality of the Covenant and of the commandments" (82).

In chapter three, the Pope develops a further consideration: "The unacceptability of 'teleological', 'consequentialist' and 'proportionalist' ethical theories, which deny the existence of negative moral norms regarding specific kinds of behaviour, norms which are valid without exception, is confirmed in a particularly eloquent way by Christian martyrdom" (90). If there were ways around exceptionless moral norms, many martyrs could have survived.

The encyclical affirms that in raising such martyrs "to the honour of the altars, the Church has canonised their witness and declared the truth of their judgment, according to which the love of God entails the obligation to respect his commandments, even in the most dire of circumstances, and the refusal to betray those commandments, even for the sake of saving one's life" (91).

Confronted with the encyclical's criticisms of the various ways around received teaching regarding intrinsically evil acts, dissenting theologians undoubtedly will respond that the Pope has misinterpreted them, missed them altogether, and/or found no new or convincing arguments against their views. Such responses, however, will not suffice. For, even if one granted that the encyclical's analyses and arguments from reason are inadequate, its main point and its arguments from revelation would remain intact. Its main point, in effect, is that passages such as 1 Cor. 6:9–10 mean exactly what they say: those who do certain kinds of acts, such as adultery and sexual perversion, will not inherit the Kingdom—assuming, of course, that the sin, committed with full awareness and deliberate consent, remains unrepented. The Pope makes it clear that, though the "magisterium does not intend to impose upon the faithful any particular theological system, still less a philosophical one", he "has the duty to state that some trends of theological thinking and certain philosophical affirmations are incompatible with revealed truth" (29).

Dissenting moralists, of course, will reply that the prohibitions found in Scripture are less absolute than they seem. But that reply will contradict the encyclical which, referring to "the moral commandments expressed in negative form in the Old and New Testaments", teaches: "Jesus himself reaffirms that these prohibitions allow no exceptions" (52).

No doubt that will be denied by some Scripture scholars. However, until recent times, when some Jewish and Christian theologians began denying that there are intrinsically evil acts, no Jew or Christian ever imagined that "You shall not murder, You shall not commit adultery" mean no more than that one may not kill the innocent without a proportionate reason or engage in extramarital intercourse unchastely or irresponsibly. Any attempt to interpret God's words as allowing such exceptions would imply that for millennia the moral truth which God meant to communicate was radically misunderstood—that God failed to communicate effectively. God, however, cannot have failed to communicate effectively.

Moreover, if the view that the commandments admit exceptions were correct, the whole body of believers would have been mistaken until almost today. But ever since Pentecost it has been true that the Holy Spirit is permanently present in the Church, so that "the universal body of the faithful . . . cannot be mistaken in belief . . . in matters of faith and morals" (109, quoting *Lumen Gentium* 12). Consequently, the rejection of the Pope's interpretation of Scripture is implicitly inconsistent with any Catholic conception of divine revelation and its transmission.

Those who nevertheless continue to dissent no doubt will take comfort from the fact that the encyclical never so much as mentions the magisterium's infallibility. I think, however, it would be a mistake to interpret this silence as a concession to the view that the received teaching about intrinsically evil acts falls outside the scope of infallibility. For one thing, *Donum Veritatis*, the Congregation for the Doctrine of the Faith's 1990 instruction concerning theologians' role in the Church, recalled the magisterium's infallibility not only in general but also specifically in moral matters. The present encyclical, in the passage quoted just above from *Lumen Gentium* 12, refers, though without using the word, to the infallability of the whole Church in matters of morals.

More important, however, is that John Paul II by no means weakens past claims for the authority of the moral teaching he reaffirms in this encyclical. While nowhere treating the magisterium's infallibility, he everywhere teaches that the exceptionlessness of the relevant norms is a revealed truth—that is, a truth demanding from every Catholic the assent of faith. Thus, the appeal is to God's authority in revealing, which is the source of the Church's infallibility in believing and the magisterium's authority in teaching.

Theologians who have been dissenting from the doctrine reaffirmed in this encyclical now have only three choices: to admit that they have been mistaken, to admit that they do not believe God's word, or to claim that the Pope is grossly misinterpreting the Bible. No doubt, many will make the third choice. In doing so, they will greatly escalate the conflict which has divided the Catholic Church during the past thirty years.

In claiming that the received teaching concerning intrinsically evil acts is a revealed truth, the Pope also implicitly asserts that it is definable. That implicit assertion will be denied by those rejecting the teaching. This argument is undeniably over essentials, and cannot long go unresolved. It cannot be settled by theologians. Only the magisterium's definitive judgment will settle it.

A distrust that wounds

Bernhard Häring

After reading the new papal encyclical carefully, I felt greatly discouraged. Several hours later I suffered long-lasting seizures of the brain, and looked forward hopefully to leaving the Church on earth for the Church in heaven. After regaining my normal brain function, however, I have a new feeling of confidence, without blinding my eyes and heart to the pain and brain-convulsions that are likely to ensue in the immediate future.

Veritatis Splendor contains many beautiful things. But almost all real splendour is lost when it becomes evident that the whole document is directed above all towards one goal: to endorse total assent and submission to all utterances of the Pope, and above all on one crucial point: that the use of any artificial means for regulating birth is intrinsically evil and sinful, without exception, even in circumstances where contraception would be a lesser evil.

The Pope is confident that he has a binding duty to proclaim his teachings with no calculation whatsoever about the foreseeable practical consequences for the people concerned and for the whole

Church. He would consider such considerations unlawful and dangerous, because they take into account a weighing of values. Whatever the risk, whatever the danger, he believes that his insights brook no dissent, but can be met only with obedience.

The recent *Catechism of the Catholic Church* issued with the Pope's authority shows that he does acknowledge that negative precepts allow of exceptions. For example, the prohibition against killing can be set aside in cases of self-defence, exaction of the death penalty, and even just wars. For him, the wrongness of contraception is much more absolute than the commandment, "Thou shalt not kill".

What about the negative precept proclaimed by the Lord himself to all his disciples, "You are not to swear at all" (Mt.5:34)? In this case not only does the Pope allow exceptions, but imposes them as a rule on whole groups of members of the Church.

There is here a striking difference between our Pope today and John Paul I, who before his election had for many years been an outstanding teacher of moral theology. As Albino Luciani, he had suggested a change of doctrine; then when Paul VI in his encyclical *Humanae Vitae* reiterated the ban on contraception, he decided to keep silent. Soon after his election as Pope, however, he left no doubt that he would propose a review of the teaching, with emphasis on a consultative approach (cf. Camillo Bassoto, *Il mio cuore è a Venezia*, Albino Luciani, Venice, 1990). Although he had given much attention to the issue, he never felt such a confidence in his own competence as to remove the need to listen patiently to all concerned and to engage in dialogue with theologians and bishops. As a moral theologian John Paul I shared fully the conviction of the vast majority of moral theologians of the past and of the present that it is unlawful and possibly a great injustice to impose on people heavy burdens in the name of God unless it is fully clear that this really is God's will.

John Paul II's mentality is different. His starting point is a high sense of duty, combined with absolute trust in his own competence, with the special assistance of the Holy Spirit. And this absolute trust in his own powers is coupled with a profound distrust towards all theologians (particularly moral theologians) who might not be in total sympathy with him.

In *Veritatis Splendor* John Paul II makes no secret that he has for a number of years felt driven to write an encyclical to bring theologians into line with his teaching on sexual morals, particularly on contraception. Yet he trusts moral theologians like Carlo Caffarra who organised a congress of other "trustworthy" moralists and produced the incredible assertion that the Church until 1917 considered contraception, whether within marriage or outside it, as "murder". Caffarra was referring to the *Corpus Juris Canonici* which only said that "those who afflict men or women with magical means or poison so that they become unable to procreate, to conceive or to give birth to a child, and do so inspired by hate or enmity, should be considered as murderers". Caffarra is still head of the John Paul II Institute in Rome, despite such incredible use of church documents.

The Pope's approach has been expressed in many talks and disciplinary measures. It has been expressed also in structures:

1. The new code of canon law criminalises dissent (canon 1371, number 1). Anyone who is admonished for an utterance and does not declare full assent, commits a punishable crime. Not the slightest possibility is admitted of doing so with a good, sincere conscience. This text was introduced at the last moment by the Pope without any consultation of the international commission which prepared the new code.

2. There is complete central control of nominations of all theologians, including moral theologians, teaching in church-related institutions at the higher level. For the controllers, no doubt, the heart of the matter is that any theologian, to be approved, must give the fullest assent to all papal pronouncements about contraception and similar questions.

3. To a large extent, a similar control operates over the nominations of bishops and other office-holders in the Church.

4. When the previous three measures did not work perfectly, the next step was to require a new form of confession of faith, including now whole-hearted assent to non-infallible (that is, fallible) papal teaching, and a particular oath of fidelity towards the supreme pontiff. The *Acta Apostolicae Sedis* say that this measure was approved by the *Sanctissimus* (Most Holy). The text speaks of the Pope as *Beatissimus* (Most Blessed). Should one see

some special significance in that? Do not these titles given to the Pope sacralise his authority unduly?

5. It is by now well known that papal agencies take enormous trouble to find out who is "trustworthy" and who is not. And who has the say in this process? What role does assent to papal sexual ethics play?

6. Now comes the encyclical *Veritatis Splendor*. Its words will press hard on the consciences of all who might be concerned, though clearly the Pope and his special adviser do not have a proper picture of what moral theology today is like. Very grave insinuations are made. What moral theologian of good reputation in the Church would recognise himself in the picture which *Veritatis Splendor* draws?

The Pope's objective is to fulfil in this way the mission entrusted by Christ to Peter and his successors: "You must lend strength to your brothers" (Lk. 22:32). But these words must be set in their immediate context. Peter assures his master and fellow disciples: "Everyone else may fall away, but I will not" (Mk. 14:29). The Lord warns him against this self-confidence and says: "I have prayed that your faith may not fail. When you have been converted, you must lend strength to your brothers." It is clear from this what conversion means for Peter. It is also clear how he should strengthen his brothers.

Peter's downfall came from his inability to believe in a humble, suffering and non-violent Servant-Messiah. Having been converted, the main task of Peter, and of all who join him, is to confess and to profess through the witness of their whole lives that the Father has raised to life and exalted to glory his suffering Servant, Jesus Christ. There is surely nothing whatsoever in this text that could be taken as relating to a task laid on Peter to teach his brothers about an absolute norm forbidding in every case any kind of contraception. Nor did Jesus tell Peter to teach a complete set of norms and laws to be fulfilled by everyone, including negative laws constraining everyone. Was not Peter wavering about whether the new Christian converts should observe Jewish law? Did not Paul have to confront him and set him right about this?

The Pope is aware that the vast majority of married people are unable to fall into full agreement with the absolute ban on contraception, that they resist the emphasis with which it is inculcated, and cannot follow the arguments by which it is justified. Most moral theologians, probably, are of the same mind. The papal response to this public opinion in the Church is not new but is now delivered with a new emphasis: the Church is not democratic, but hierarchical. Let us ask our Pope: are you sure your confidence in your supreme human, professional and religious competence in matters of moral theology and particularly sexual ethics is truly justified?

As to contraception, there is no word on the subject anywhere in divine revelation. This is a matter of what we call the natural law written deep in the hearts of men and women, and therefore we must and can find a fruitful approach which is appropriate. Since natural law is "open to the eyes of reason", we should reason together gently and patiently as we consider the case "on either side" (Rom. 2:12, 16). The hierarchical constitution of the Church cannot in the least contradict or disallow this approach in any matter which concerns the law written in our hearts and calling for a response from our consciences.

Away with all distrust in our Church! Away with all attitudes, mentalities and structures which promote it! We should let the Pope know that we are wounded by the many signs of his rooted distrust, and discouraged by the manifold structures of distrust which he has allowed to be established. We need him to soften towards us, the whole Church needs it. Our witness to the world needs it. The urgent call to effective ecumenism needs it.

Let me suggest, for a start, one healing and encouraging event. Let the Vatican destroy all its lists—I have seen one of them—of those who are considered "trustworthy" ("*affidabili*") and of those who are not, simply as regards this one issue of the absolute wrongness of artificial contraception. The Church has greater concerns than this, more urgent needs: to proclaim the good news and to encourage all to set out on the road to holiness.

And let us honour God's gracious forgiveness by forgiving each other for the harm we have inflicted on each other and the anger we may have harboured in our hearts.

Killing the patient

Richard McCormick

The encyclical *Veritatis Splendor*, signed on 6 August but released on 5 October, did not appear from nowhere, a kind of surprising and sudden ecclesial "Big Bang" documented. The temperature had been elevating gradually but perceptibly.

In 1983 Cardinal Edouard Gagnon, now president of the prestigious Pontifical Committee for International Eucharistic Congresses, proposed an intriguing "final solution" for the moral problems of our times: "change 90 per cent of the teachers of moral theology and stop them from teaching". That is quite remarkable therapy. But what is the disease?

If one is allowed a mischievous suspicion, one might suggest that Cardinal Gagnon and Cardinal Joseph Ratzinger have occasionally shared a coffee over the subject. For in the *Ratzinger Report*—a summary of some interviews in 1984—Ratzinger identified the disease, at least in the moral sphere, as "consequentialism" and "proportionalism" and saw it as infecting especially American moral theologians. This conveniently overlooked the fact that the major contributors to this tendency were European (Peter Knauer SJ, Bruno Schüller SJ, Josef Fuchs SJ, Louis Janssens, the late Franz Böckle, and Franz Scholtz, to name but a few). Whatever the case, there can be little doubt that the impulse towards *Veritatis Splendor* has been building up for some time. Indeed, there is absolutely nothing new in the heart of the encyclical that had not been stated earlier.

In his apostolic exhortation *Reconciliatio et Paenitentia* (2 December 1984), John Paul II gave strong hints as to what would appear in *Veritatis Splendor*. In the 1984 document he deplored the loss of the sense of sin in our time. He listed several influences that undermine this sense. One such influence he identified as a "system of ethics". (Another noted was the notion of the fundamental option. I cannot treat it here since it is a complicated subject.) The Pope stated: "This may take the form of an ethical system which relativizes the moral norm, denying its absolute and unconditional value, and as a consequence denying that there can be intrinsically illicit acts, independent of the circumstances in which they are performed by the subject." He was, I believe, ill served by his advisers in framing the matter in this way.

Equivalently the Pope is saying that certain actions can be morally wrong from the object (*ex objecto*) independently of circumstances. As the German theologian, Bruno Schüller SJ, one of the most influential of proportionalists, has shown, that is analytically obvious *if the object is characterized in advance as morally wrong*. No theologian would or could contest the papal statement understood in that sense. But it is not the issue. The key problem is: what objects should be characterized as morally wrong and on what criteria? Of course, hidden in this question is the further one: what is to count as pertaining to the object? That is often decided by an independent ethical judgment about what one thinks is morally right or wrong in certain areas.

Let the term "lie" serve as an example here. The Augustinian-Kantian approach holds that every falsehood is a lie. Others would hold that falsehood is morally wrong (a lie) only when it is denial of the truth to one who has a right to know. In the first case the object of the act is said to be falsehood (= lie) and it is seen as *ex objecto* morally wrong. In the second case the object is "falsehood to protect an important secret" and is seen as *ex objecto* morally right (*ex objecto* because the very end must be viewed as pertaining to the object).

If you are with me so far, hang on. Here is more. These differing judgments do not trace to disagreements about the fonts of morality (object, end, circumstances), but to different judgments about the use of human speech. Some view "falsehood to protect a secret" as permissible, others do not. In this sense one could fully agree with the Pope that there are "intrinsically illicit acts independent of the circumstances" and yet deny that this applies to the very matters apparently of the most concern to him (sterilization, contraception, masturbation). The quite traditional Jesuit author of a popular manual of moral theology, H. Noldin, wrote:

> All those things pertain to the object of the act that constitute its *substance*, viewed not physically but *morally*; furthermore, all those things constitute the substance of an act which are so essential and necessary to it that if something is lacking or added, the act is different. Thus, the object of theft is someone's property taken against his reasonable will; for if the thing is not someone else's, or is taken with the owner's consent or not against his reasonable opposition, it is not theft.

Take masturbation, for instance. When masturbation occurs in the context of sperm testing, there are many theologians who believe that this context enters the very object or meaning of the act. In other words, they regard it as an act different from self-pleasuring, much as they would think killing in self-defence is a different act from killing during a robbery. Those who reject these differences have attributed a full independent moral character to the material event of self-stimulation that they do not attribute to the merely material event of "speaking falsehood" or "taking another's property".

But now to *Veritatis Splendor*. The encyclical is divided into three parts. Chapter one is a biblical meditation on Jesus' dialogue with the rich young man (Mt. 19: 16–22). Chapter two critically reviews certain trends in contemporary moral theology. Chapter three addresses the importance of Christian morality for the life of the Church and world and especially the teaching responsibility of bishops.

Two brief introductory remarks. First, I must note a problem. In its key second chapter, *Veritatis Splendor* is dense and technical. The Pope has joined an in-house conversation among moral theologians. To deal with the encyclical adequately, one has to plough through some heavy theological literature and language. Very frankly, few non-specialists will read the papal letter, and of those who do most will emerge with cluttered and clouded but not clear heads. I state this by way of apology for the commentary that follows.

Secondly, all Catholic moral theologians should and will welcome the beautiful Christ-centred presentation unfolded in chapter one and the ringing rejection of the false dichotomies identified by John Paul II: between autonomy and theonomy, freedom and law, conscience and truth, and the rest. These extreme positions come to a dead end in relativism, subjectivism, and individualism, and all of us repudiate such pathologies. But many theologians will protest that their work has nothing to do with these deviations.

That brings us to one of the tendencies that concerns that Pope: proportionalism. It is impossible in a brief space to give a fair summary of the developments that are described by the term "proportionalism" or an adequate account of the differences that individual theologians bring to their analyses. Common to all so-called proportionalists, however, is the insistence that causing certain disvalues (nonmoral, pre-moral evils such as sterilization, deception in speech, wounding and violence) in our conduct does not by that very fact make the action morally wrong, as certain traditional formulations supposed. These evils or disvalues are said to be premoral when considered abstractly, that is, in isolation from their morally relevant circumstances. But they are evils. Thus theologians sometimes say that they are morally relevant, but not morally decisive. They are morally relevant because they ought to be avoided as far as possible. The action in which they occur becomes morally wrong when, all things considered, there is not a proportionate reason in the act justifying the disvalue. Thus, just as not every killing is murder, not every falsehood is a lie, so not every artificial intervention preventing or promoting conception in marriage is necessarily an unchaste act.

Now let us turn to the papal letter. There we read, of proportionalism: "Such theories are not faithful to the Church's teaching, when they believe they can justify, as morally good, deliberate choices of kinds of behaviour contrary to the commandments of the divine and natural law" (76). Later in 81 we read: "If acts are intrinsically evil, a good intention or particular circumstances can diminish their evil, but they cannot remove it." In brief, the encyclical repeatedly states of proportionalism that it attempts to justify morally wrong actions by a good intention. This, I regret to say, is a misrepresentation.

I wish the Pope's advisers had been more careful here. No proportionalist that I know would recognize himself or herself in that description. The stated objection is not new. It has been discussed—and I believe successfully rebutted—for many years. I shall try to summarize here what I believe is really going on in some recent work. I realize that the matter is heavy rowing. But here goes.

In the past some have objected that certain actions are (and have been taught by the magisterium to be) morally wrong *ex objecto* (from the object). But proportionalists, it is asserted, do not and cannot say this since they insist on looking at all dimensions of the act before saying it is morally wrong. The acts in question are such as contraception and masturbation.

What is to be said of this objection (and remember, it is the Pope's objection)? I think it misses the point of what proportionalists are saying. When contemporary theologians say that certain disvalues in our actions can be justified by a proportionate reason, they are not saying that *morally wrong actions (ex objecto)* can be justified by the end. They are saying that an action cannot be judged morally wrong simply by looking at the material happening, or at its object in a very narrow and restricted sense. This is precisely what tradition has done in certain categories (contraception and sterilization, for instance). It does this in no other area.

If we want to put this in traditional categories (object, end, circumstances), we can say that the tradition has defined certain actions as morally wrong *ex objecto* because it has included in the object not simply the material happening (object in a very narrow sense) but also elements beyond it which clearly exclude any possible justification. Thus, a theft is not simply "taking another's property", but doing so "against the reasonable will of the owner". This latter addition has two characteristics in the tradition. (1) It is considered as essential to the object. (2) It excludes any possible exceptions. Why? Because if a person is in extreme difficulty and needs food, the owner is not reasonably unwilling that his food be taken. Fair enough. Yet, when the same tradition deals with, for example, masturbation or sterilization, it adds little or nothing to the material happening and regards such a materially described act alone as constituting the object. If it were consistent, it would describe the object as "sterilization *against the good of marriage*". This all could accept.

Let me return, then, to John Paul II's language. He cites as an objection to proportionalist tendencies the notion that some acts are intrinsically evil from their object. I believe all proportionalists would admit this *if the object is broadly understood as including all the morally relevant circumstances.*

In conclusion, proportionalists are not justifying "deliberate choices of kinds of behaviour contrary to the commands of the divine and natural law". They are saying that we must look at all dimensions (morally relevant circumstances) before we know what the action is and whether it should be said to be "contrary to the commands of the divine and natural law".

My own reading of this encyclical letter suggests that an item on the agenda is unstated. It is this. I am convinced that the Pope will reject a priori any analytic adjustments in moral theology that do not support the moral wrongfulness of every contraceptive act. Proportionalism certainly does not give such support.

What will be the effect of this encyclical letter? On the public, zero. It is too technical and abstract to address anyone but specialists. How about bishops? Chapter three urges bishops to take their teaching responsibilities seriously. Will that mean refusing a forum to theologians who disagree here and there with an official judgment (usually on a matter of concrete application where disagreement should, according to Vatican II and the American bishops as well, be expected)? Nothing new here. It has been going on for years. Will it mean sackings from teaching positions? Hardly and for two reasons. First, the bishops will wisely (I hope) want to maintain the credibility of Catholic higher education by supporting its institutional autonomy.

Secondly, the vast majority of moral theologians known as proportionalists will *rightly* say that they do not hold or teach what the encyclical attributes to them. They cannot be punished for uncommitted crimes. In this respect *Veritatis Splendor* differs from Pius XII's *Humani Generis* (1950). Pius's encyclical sadly led to silencings and sackings (Yves Congar, Henri de Lubac, Jean Daniélou, *et al.*). Most of the positions of these distinguished theologians were eventually accepted by the Church at Vatican II. *Veritatis Splendor* at key points attributes to theologians positions that they do not hold. It will, I predict, eventually enjoy an historical status similar to *Humani Generis*.

4

Good acts and good persons

Josef Fuchs

St Augustine tied himself in knots attempting to explain why, though even venial sins conflict with God's will, not all sins are equally mortal. Many moral theologians today say the problem is not so much theological as anthropological, because it touches the depths of the human person. To deal with it, they have developed the theory of the "fundamental option", as it is called. But this approach is not universal in the Church. Some theologians do not take seriously this complex of problems, if indeed they consider them at all. They betray themselves by the paucity of their writings on the topic.

The encyclical *Veritatis Splendor* (nos. 65–70) addresses the question in very critical fashion. For the most part it hews close to the line laid down by the 1984 apostolic exhortation, *Reconciliatio et Paenitentia*, and the 1975 declaration of the Congregation for the Doctrine of the Faith, *Persona Humana*. But the encyclical does not mention this declaration.

The theory of a "fundamental option" goes back mainly to the development by the late Karl Rahner SJ of ideas borrowed from Jacques Maritain and Joseph Maréchal SJ. Rahner's preferred term was not in fact "fundamental option" but "the human person's disposition of his self as a whole". Without some such theory, Rahner maintained, many church statements on dogmatic or fundamental theology and above all on moral theology were unintelligible.

The theory does not aim to deal with practical questions. Rather, it focuses on a more thorough understanding of the theological and anthropological depths of the human person as the subject of moral action. So the preoccupation with the distinction between mortal and venial sins found in the Vatican documents of 1975 and 1984 and to some extent in *Veritatis Splendor* misses the point, as we shall see later.

As understood by its proponents, among whom I include myself, the theory goes something like this. Human freedom is one single reality—but its effects occur in two different but related spheres. On the one hand, we experience freedom in everyday moral choices: here the person, more or less free, chooses the most morally significant actions. On the other hand, in such decisions about particular actions, already the person commits himself as a whole, as a person: hence one can talk of *fundamental* freedom. Thus, not only are the person's particular actions good or bad, but also the person himself as a whole.

Whereas freedom of choice is encountered within our reflective conscious experience, this is not true of the fundamental freedom. In order to be aware of it consciously and as an object, a person would have to be able to stand outside himself in order to inspect himself, but the self as a whole cannot do that. So awareness of *fundamental* freedom is not directly accessible to observation and verification. Necessarily a-thematic (that is, not conceptual and not reflectively conscious), it is also termed "transcendental", echoing what St Thomas says in speaking of the person as *present* to himself (*Summa Theologiae* I.67.1; *Summa contra Gentiles* 4.11).

So one may say that a person, in terms of fundamental freedom, has his own ethical quality—that is, a person may be good or evil; it is not just his *actions* that come under moral

22

judgement as right or wrong. The ethical *fundamental option* made by the person, based on his fundamental freedom, is not itself a single *act* of self-disposition, though it is always felt *in* (though not *through*) particular acts of deciding. Rather than act, it is best seen as a process towards an ethical disposition which can grow or decline.

The fundamental option is expressed in decisions about individual actions, exercised with free choice. It influences them, while also being influenced by them. This reciprocal relation between the fundamental option and freedom of choice has certain consequences, according to those who defend this view.

First, it is just not possible for us to examine the core of our person from the outside so as to establish whether we are fundamentally good or evil—or rather, since we can only be good through grace, whether we are living in God's grace and love. What we *can* know about good and evil is limited to our actions, decisions and desires. But—as St Thomas puts it—we can also to some extent conclude by a conjecture based on our actions (*per coniecturam, Summa Theologiae* I-I.112.5c) whether we really are as persons good or evil: that is, whether we are bound firmly in God's grace and love or not.

A second consequence follows. Since the fundamental ethical option goes so much deeper than particular ethical choices about concrete actions, it is not as easy for a good person to change his of her fundamental option as it would be to swap morally good particular actions for morally bad ones, as St Thomas explicitly says (*De Veritate* 27.1. ad. 9).

Finally, individual decisions and actions that may be called "peripheral" (that is, not substantially penetrated by the central fundamental option) can nevertheless gradually bring a person to a point at which he is now committed to the contrary of his previous direction and disposition. When this happens, his fundamental option is reversed.

The critical assessment of the theory of the "fundamental option" found in *Veritatis Splendor* suggests that the Pope's theological advisers have not understood deeply enough the thought-world of Karl Rahner and with the widespread development of the theory among moral theologians and others. Manifestly, they do not grasp that the fundamental option and everyday moral choices happen on different levels of the same person, and so cannot be categorized on the same level of objective awareness.

The papal consultors do indeed know about the way a host of personal basic inclinations can provide, as it were, a river-bed for everyday particular decisions to run along (65). They even find such fundamental tendencies in the Bible (66). But for them all this belongs to the objective realm of the ethical consciousness of the person. They do not see it as the necessarily a-thematic (that is, not conceptually conscious) reality present at the core of the person.

In this way the fundamental option as defined by its protagonists is misunderstood in the encyclical. In its negative and therefore sinful form, this option is seen by the encyclical as the "explicit and formal rejection of God and one's neighbour"; and it is presented as though it were a precise, definite and determinable *act* (69). I know no proponent of the fundamental option who has said this. The encyclical's theologians *assume* that ethical judgement on a person can be delivered solely on the basis of his conscious and free decisions about individual acts (67).

When they criticize the theory of the "fundamental option", these consultors see a split or dissociation between the fundamental option, on the one hand, and the individual acts, on the other (111 and 66), which in their view drags those acts down and would make them insignificant as far as the person is concerned (65). In truth, precisely because the fundamental option and moral choices are on different levels, the theory stresses rather their mutual relationship and interpenetration, and thus is the very contrary of division and separation.

The encyclical attacks the idea that the moral quality of individual acts may be determined only by the intention and the fundamental option of the person concerned (67). Then it states that every particular act involves some reference to good or evil. But who would wish to deny this? The problem is how this relates to the ethical status of the person as a whole, which is on another level.

A similar comment applies when the encyclical asserts that the fundamental option can sometimes be determined by a particular action or even overthrown by it (67 and 70). Yet how can decisions on the objective and conceptual level determine the personal inaccessible "fundamental option" unless they attain to the same non-conceptual level? Likewise, the possibility is calmly envisaged of people going to their eternal damnation on the basis of grave sins (88) without having a personal fundamental option. To repeat: the fundamental option is not an individual act, and particular serious sins do not lead as such to eternal damnation unless embodied in a fundamental option to reject God. For at the end of the road of genuinely free acts, there remains only the sinner as he or she is. At this point, in the furthest depths of the person, the fundamental option becomes a final option.

The International Theological Commission (ITC) got it right in its 1982 declaration on reconciliation and conversion: "According to the teaching of the Church, the *fundamental decision* ultimately determines the ethical constitution of the human person. But the concept of fundamental decision cannot provide an everyday *criterion* for distinguishing between serious and non-serious sins. Its purpose is rather to make clear what serious sin is.

"True, the human person may be able to express or alter his or her (fundamental) decision *in* (my italics) an individual act, provided the act is undertaken consciously and freely; but this does not mean that every particular act involves the entire fundamental decision, or that each individual sin must *ipso facto* be a revocation of the fundamental decision" (published in, for example, *Internationale Zeitschrift Communio* 13, 1984, pp. 44–63).

Veritatis Splendor is in fact very restrained when it comes to clear condemnation of any of the schools of moral theology. For instance, in the formulation of no. 70 the encyclical says, using the conditional, that the fundamental option should be rejected "if it is understood in such a way that at the objective level it alters or puts in doubt the traditional concept of mortal sin". The theory certainly does not do that. On the contrary, it deepens the sense of mortal sin.

At the end of the encyclical the Pope turns his gaze towards moral theologians. He makes a modest request for help which seems clearly to point in a precise direction. He says: "While recognizing the possible limitations of the human arguments employed by the magisterium, moral theologians are called to develop a deeper understanding of the reasons underlying its teachings." But there can be no guarantee in advance—as moral theologians and presumably the Pope all know very well—that moral theologians will be successful in doing so.

5

Teaching in crisis

Nicholas Lash

The slightly nervous respect with which the papal encyclical *Veritatis Splendor* has been received in circles not known either for their affection for the Catholic Church or for their approval of authoritarian government is, I think, evidence of two things: the towering public stature of the present Pope and the recognition that the moral crisis of our time is every bit as grave and comprehensive as he supposes it to be.

Consider our circumstances: the collapse of Communism, coinciding with diminishing confidence in the ideals and visions of the project of Enlightenment, as nineteenth-century dreams of progress fade into late twentieth-century self-doubt; the spreading disillusion with democratic politics; the confusion in regard to family life and questions of sex and gender; the degeneration of cities into wildernesses of poverty and squalor punctuated by fortresses of wealth; the conflict of old tribalisms crumbling the brittle surface of the nation state; the rape of non-renewable resources for short-term gain; the apparently final victory of what

Karl Marx deplored as the "universalization of the commodity form", with price the only value and pleasure the only goal; and, as the global context of it all, the cries of dying children in that larger part of humankind whose subordination to our flourishing we sanitize with reference to "our markets". It is not surprising that when the Pope speaks of "an ever more widespread and acute sense of the need for a radical personal and social renewal capable of ensuring justice, solidarity, honesty and openness" (98) as the only way to avoid "a headlong plunge into the most dangerous crisis which can afflict man: the confusion between good and evil" (93), he wins a hearing.

In such a situation, a pope might exercise his leadership of the episcopate by enlisting his brother bishops' help in bringing the riches of Catholic scholarship and pastoral experience to bear upon our moral dilemmas. By God's grace and through our common labour, truth's splendour might thereby illuminate a little the darkness of our time. To this end, he might issue an encyclical: brief, specific, concrete, identifying the agenda of our moral task. Pope John Paul II has, however, written an encyclical of a different kind, with different purposes in mind.

The first of the three chapters of *Veritatis Splendor*, which has already been widely welcomed and admired, is an extended meditation on the dialogue, in Matthew 19, between Jesus and the rich young man.

Weaving in Aquinas's classic definition of "natural law" as "nothing other than the light of understanding infused in us by God, whereby we understand what must be done and what must be avoided" (12), and presenting the commandments as not a "minimum limit" but rather as "the first necessary step on the journey towards freedom" (15, 13), the Pope integrates precepts and counsels into a single story of the human journey, enabled, drawn and coaxed by God, through holiness towards eternal life. The vision which he sketches here shines out against the darker tones, in Chapter three, of a world in which, with the sinews which should bind together truth, goodness and freedom slackened and almost lost from view, the vocation of all Christians to uncompromising obedience to truth finds sharpest focus in the witness of the martyrs.

The lengthy second chapter is in quite different language. With very little said about the following of Christ, it operates for the most part in the territory of natural law, now no longer understood (as St Thomas did) as God's illumination of our hearts and minds—as, we might say, a Christian account of what makes human behaviour *moral* action—but rather (in the manner of the nineteenth-century text-books) as a kind of *code*, a manual of law, "laying down" (see 50), often in great detail, what we should and should not do. As the author issues dire warnings against dangerous and erroneous tendencies with long names like "proportionalism" and "teleologism", it becomes increasingly clear that, far from being a general treatment of "certain fundamental questions of the Church's moral teaching", the encyclical has one central and overriding aim (correctly identified by Professor Grisez in his essay): "the reaffirmation of the universality and immutability of the moral commandments, particularly those which prohibit always and without exception intrinsically evil acts" (115). And it is not war or poverty, atheism or the dead hand of the "commodity form", which most preoccupies the Pope, but sex.

This may not be immediately apparent because the Pope cites, as examples of intrinsically evil acts, a catalogue, from Vatican II's constitution on the Church in the modern world, *Gaudium et Spes*, of practices which the Council condemned as disgraceful and a denial of the honour due to God. The list includes: "any kind of homicide, genocide, abortion . . . deportation, slavery, prostitution . . . degrading conditions of work which treat labourers as mere instruments of profit" (80), and so on.

Few of these practices, however, can easily be made to fit the Pope's description, worked out with such care and defended with such vigour, of intrinsically evil acts. Thus, for example, the assertion that "any kind of homicide" is intrinsically evil would be either false or tautologous. Tautologous, if "any kind of homicide" means any kind of killing that is not permitted; false, if homicide simply means killing human beings. "When it is a matter of the moral norms prohibiting intrinsic evil, there are no privileges or exceptions for anyone" (96). Yet Catholic tradition has been flexible enough for popes and bishops to have tolerated—sometimes through silence, sometimes through connivance—most of the slaughter of two world wars and the killing fields of Vietnam. Pope John Paul II's reiterated and outspoken opposition to modern war is admirable, but beside the point. The lists (referred to by Professor Häring in his essay) of those deemed "trustworthy" for ecclesiastical promotion seem not to be confined to pacifists.

The case of slavery is rather different. The encyclical lays great emphasis on the "unchanging" character of "the precepts prohibiting intrinsically evil acts" (95). Yet it is only in the last 200 years, in response to pressures from outside the Church, that slavery has been condemned outright as wicked. Quoting the new *Catechism of the Catholic Church* to the effect that St Paul told Philemon to treat his slave as a brother (see 100) is no help here. If Paul had considered slavery intrinsically evil, he would have instructed Philemon to liberate Onesimus forthwith, for there is no privilege or exception in these matters.

The point is that it is neither homicide nor slavery that the Pope has in his sights. In saying this, I am not denying that it is the whole culture of moral relativism—the determination of right and wrong by private preference or public power—against which he courageously takes his stand. In that sense, those commentators are correct who insist that this encyclical is about much more than sex. Nevertheless, the theory of human acts in which his case is grounded, and to which he attends in such detail, is one whose chief use in recent years has been to attempt so to specify the "object" of contraceptive acts as to render them analogous—in their absolutely exceptionless objective immorality—not to homicide, or slavery, or deportation, but to murder. Thus it is not, in fact, at all surprising that, immediately after the long list quoted from *Gaudium et Spes*, comes what is perhaps the most embarrassing sentence in the encyclical: "With regard to intrinsically evil acts, and in reference to contraceptive practices . . . Pope Paul VI teaches" (80; there follows a quotation from *Humanae Vitae*). This sentence is embarrassing because Pope Paul VI did not say that contraception was intrinsically evil (*malum*) but intrinsically "*inhonestum*".[1] And the one thing clear about the meaning of this word is that it was chosen in order to *avoid* saying "*malum*". Which would seem to make the phrase "With regard to . . ." tendentious.

(Incidentally, I cannot see what would be lost by rendering "*malum*" as "bad", which has a greater range of sense than "evil".)

Pope John Paul insists that "the Church's magisterium does not intend to impose upon the faithful any particular theological system, still less a philosophical one" (29). In which case, it must be possible for his timely insistence that truth's splendour—shining in the face of Christ and, in the Spirit's gift, in human minds and hearts—is not our plaything or arbitrary creation, to be expressed in different imaginative frameworks and with recourse to different styles of argument. And yet the encyclical appears to argue that the richness and integrity of traditional Catholic ethics is adequately represented by only one school of moral philosophy (itself a by-product of the rationalist temper of early modern culture) whose intellectual habits, insensitive to literary, exegetical or historical considerations, generate a style of moral thinking far removed from the common sense of an Aquinas, who prefaced his treatise on the virtues with the sensibly Aristotelean reminder that generalizations in matters of ethics are of minimal utility because actions are particular.

According to Pope John Paul, there is a "genuine crisis" (5) in the Church, a crisis brought about by certain "trends" in moral thinking which are "systematically calling into question . . . traditional moral doctrine" (4). These trends, catalogued in Chapter two, seem to embrace all schools of Catholic thought save that one through whose mindset these others are (and not without distortion) viewed. At the very least, it is difficult to reconcile the Pope's assurance that he does not seek to impose theological or philosophical uniformity with the fact that he neither praises nor commends any school or style, approach or method, other than his own.

I am not a moral theologian but, from my position in nearby territory, conversation between this one school of moral theology and all the rest seems to have deteriorated (especially in the United States) into a dialogue of the deaf. I would not in the least dispute Professor Grisez's contention that "the argument is undeniably over essentials", but would judge the cause of truth better served by the Pope taking a leaf out of his predecessor Paul V's book and decreeing, as the latter did in 1607 in regard to the no less bitter dispute *de auxiliis*, that neither side should pronounce the contrary teaching to be heretical, than by himself acting as a spokesman for one party.

Among the more baleful features of early modern rationalism (by which Catholic thought and teaching were more deeply infected than, for a long time, we appreciated) was the dissociation of "fact" from "value", the religious expression of which was the separation, in the seventeenth century, of "moral" from "dogmatic" theology. The encyclical's insistence that moral theology is, indeed, theology, and the appeal to the conciliar requirement that moral theology should "increasingly [be] based on the teaching of Scripture (29), are thus warmly to be welcomed.[2]

It therefore follows, as a number of commentators on the encyclical have already pointed out, that the proper context for the reception and assessment of its central claims and arguments is the Church's teaching on divine revelation. Happily, that teaching has recently found expression at the most authoritative level known to Catholic tradition: namely, a dogmatic constitution of a general council; in this case, Vatican II's Constitution *Dei Verbum*.

There remains, of course, the difficulty, in these days of inexorable scholarly specialisation, that few moral theologians have the training, erudition or experience that would (from their side) facilitate the desired reintegration of Catholic ethics into the mainstream of biblical and doctrinal interpretation. This difficulty is by no means insuperable. The disciplined acknowledgement of limited competence is a necessary condition of professional conduct in any field, and requires of all of us that judgements issued outside our particular fields of expertise are moderated by the tentativeness and docility that become the amateur.

Towards the end of the encyclical, the Pope argues that, while "exchanges and conflicts of opinion may constitute normal expressions of public life in a representative democracy, moral teaching . . . is in no way established by following the rules and deliberative procedures typical of a democracy" (113). This point (though councils and similar assemblies vote) may be readily conceded. It hardly follows, however, that disagreement has no place within the Church. How else, from the dawning of the human mind, has truth been ascertained, mistakes corrected, confusion clarified, *except* through properly conducted disagreement? And yet, surprisingly, the Pope makes no mention of the role of disagreement, or of the duty of episcopal authority to monitor and guide it. Instead, he moves directly to denounce "dissent" and "opposition to the teaching of the Church's pastors" (113), as if there were not, on many of the questions that he has considered, no little disagreement within the episcopate itself.

If there is, indeed, a crisis today in Catholic teaching, then its character is clearly indicated by that bleakly authoritarian final paragraph (113) of the section on "the service of moral theologians". This crisis has arisen, in part, because the two dogmatic constitutions of Vatican II, on the Church and on Revelation, left unresolved a dangerous modern imprecision in uses of the term "*magisterium*". (Of twenty-five occurrences of the term in *Veritatis Splendor*, no less than nine are to be found in the short section on the service of moral theologians.)

Christianity *is* a kind of teaching: a people whose identity consists in hearing, responding to, embodying, proclaiming, the *message* that is God's living Word. It is, then, not surprising that questions concerning the office and function of Christian teachership, or "*magisterium*", should be deemed of paramount importance.

Catholic tradition has never underestimated the special burden of responsibility borne by the episcopate in protecting the integrity of teaching in the Church but, of course, the function is very widely exercised. Parents, teachers, pastors, theologians—all, in different ways, formally or informally, exercise *magisterium* in the Church.

Around 1840, for the first time, the term was used to refer, not to an office, but rather to a class of officials; not to a function, but rather to a particular group of functionaries (the distinction is that which we draw, in English, between the function of "government" and what we call "the Government"). Now, of course, once the question is asked: which group in the Church are "the" teachers? which group are "the" magisterium?—the answer must be: the episcopate.

So far, so almost good (for theologians will not lose much

sleep if they no longer have one Latin term ascribed to them, descriptive of their teaching office). During the latter part of the nineteenth century, however, and especially in the twentieth, the connotations of the term shifted again until it came to refer, in fact, and without official sanction, not to the bishops of the Catholic Church but to what is known as "Rome".

To be blunt: it is not "dissent" but duty that has led me in the past, and leads me still, vigorously to protest against usages which serve as a smokescreen under cover of which responsibility for guiding and securing Catholic teaching is transferred from the episcopate to other agencies.

Near the end of the encyclical, Pope John Paul says that "this is the first time ... that the Magisterium of the Church has set forth in detail the fundamental elements of this teaching" (115). This is, in fact, and no doubt unintentionally, to contract "the magisterium" to the Pope and his advisers, and to do so in a letter written to the bishops of the Catholic Church who might well have thought that it was *they* (*cum et sub Petro*) who were "the magisterium".

It is my heartfelt plea, then, that the bishops of the Church should defuse the "crisis" of which the Pope speaks by openly and honestly (see 98) taking up the burden of their share in *magisterium*, disagreeing (if needs be) with this or that opinion of the Pope, correcting, in the name of justice and in the measure that circumstances warrant it, the account given in the letter of the teaching and intentions of moral theologians in their Churches. They will thereby contribute to that "frank and open acceptance of truth" which, according to the Pope, is "the condition for authentic freedom" (87).

Notes

1. See Peter Hebblethwaite, "Timeless Ethics", *The Tablet*, 9 October 1993, p. 1288.
2. The phrase is quoted from the Council's Decree on Priestly Formation, *Optatam Totius*, which also stipulated that the renewal of moral theology must proceed through "livelier contact with the mystery of Christ and the history of salvation" (16).

6

Truth and freedom in the thought of Pope John Paul

Maciej Zieba

I recently overheard a discussion between two professors of theology about the Pope's latest encyclical, *Veritatis Splendor*. The first, an American, admitted that it was the section on what he termed the theology of martyrdom (89–94) which seemed particularly fresh and capable of filling a gap in twentieth-century theology. But the second, a Pole, replied that this part seemed the most obvious. He himself had known and understood as a seven-year-old what the Pope was writing about now. This did not mean, he added, that Poland was a country of theological prodigies, already absorbing the Pope's teaching while still in the cradle—in reality, even among adults, Poland had trouble absorbing his teaching at all.

The Polish theologian's remark merely shows how different is the environment in which the Churches of Western Europe and Eastern Europe were brought up. Truth, loyalty to the truth, and paying the price for this loyalty—these represent the realities with which all believers, seven-year-olds included, struggled in Eastern

Europe. In this sense, the conversation I overheard has merely confirmed my view that *Veritatis Splendor* can, to some extent, be seen as a theological assessment of the experience of the Churches of Central and Eastern Europe—but an assessment particularly addressed to the Western Churches.

This hypothesis gains added legitimacy, furthermore, from the fact that the theories of the fundamental option, proportionalism and consequentialism, all of which the encyclical evaluates critically, have far fewer supporters in the theology departments of Prague, Krakow or Vilnius than in those of Tübingen, Oxford or Boston. By contrast, claims regarding the existence of an objective moral order are heard much more commonly in Eastern Europe than in the continent's Western half.

At the same time, it should be stressed that *Veritatis Splendor* is a Christian, and therefore universal, exposition of the Church's experience, rather than any transplantation of philosophical or theological thought. It manifestly and decidedly distances itself from any association with specific theological systems, let alone with any philosophical system. Indeed, the aim of avoiding reliance on some particular school was plainly one of the reasons why work on the text took seven years.

Noticing that the document most frequently cited by the Pope is Vatican II's pastoral constitution on the Church in the modern world, *Gaudium et Spes*, we can conclude that the encyclical's perspective is that of Vatican II—meaning Personalism, but with a fairly heavy metaphysical emphasis. This emerges particularly clearly from the encyclical's crucial second chapter, in which the Pope defends the unity of the person as a combination of spirit and body, and expounds his understanding of human nature.

Veritatis Splendor, then, in speaking of the universal foundations of moral theology, touches in a particular way on the situation of the Church in Western Europe and the United States. By contrast, the Pope's 1991 encyclical, *Centesimus Annus*, published to mark the anniversary of Leo XIII's social encyclical *Rerum Novarum*, expressed to a large extent the experience of the Churches living in Western democracies and was explicitly directed mainly at countries which have liberated themselves from Communism.

This probably explains why *Centesimus Annus* was received

relatively sympathetically in the United States and Western Europe, whereas, as a uniquely innovatory and difficult document, it has not been properly studied in Eastern Europe or introduced into the corpus of church social teaching there. *Centesimus Annus* gives, for the first time in history, a positive account of the free market economy, showing the good features of democracy and making suggestions as to how the Christian vocation can be fulfilled through engagement in the economic sphere.

For us in Eastern Europe, with several years' painful experience of creeping capitalism and democracy, this text is so difficult that it has simply been ignored in practice. The freedom we now experience in the political and economic sphere appears more difficult and comparatively less attractive than the abstract freedom about which we previously dreamt for years. At the same time, we in Eastern Europe share the feeling that together with freedom comes a threat to recognition of the existence of that absolute truth in which moral values are rooted. The temptation of fundamentalism is therefore increasingly attractive. In the West, on the other hand, it is not freedom but truth which brings fear. The mere recognition that absolute truth exists provokes anxieties about an explosion of intolerance and authoritarianism, and apprehension that the life of the individual will be made to conform to rigid schemes of doctrine.

The contrasting poles of freedom and truth are at the root of the problems of the contemporary world. We are afraid that absolute truth will destroy and suppress human freedom, eroding our uniqueness and trying to force our highly complex world into an anachronistic fixed pattern. But if absolute truth does *not* exist, or is unrecognizable, then even though the human being attains full autonomy, all values and every distinction between good and evil lose their universal meaning. They become mere products of culture, a question of preference, of individual taste and choice.

Having sketched out the contemporary scene, let us return to our encyclicals. *Centesimus Annus* is about freedom—but freedom, as the Pope has frequently stressed, directed towards truth—and its Christian application in social life, in politics and economic affairs. *Veritatis Splendor*, however, is first and foremost about objective truth, and about objective good and evil. Though this objectivity surpasses human involvements and circumstances, it takes account, at the same time, of human fortunes in all their complexity and, most important, is an objectivity which is open to human freedom. In John Paul II's conception, then, the polarity between freedom and truth is replaced by a dialectic between them.

For Christian life to be possible in a free world, neither truth nor freedom can demand full autonomy. Such an autonomy on the part of either could easily turn itself into tyranny. And it would then be a matter only for intellectual connoisseurs whether this was "tyranny through truth" (in the name of an ideology claiming absolute rights for itself), or "tyranny through freedom" (a threat of total anarchy resulting from the collapse of inter-personal bonds, in the name of freedom, requiring a curb to be imposed). In John Paul's approach, truth and freedom are both anti-totalitarian in character.

Another Council document which the Pope often cites in *Veritatis Splendor* is the declaration on religious freedom, which bases its argument on the principle that freedom has its foundation in human nature. The emphasis on individual freedom in *Veritatis Splendor* is complemented by the strong acceptance of political and economic freedom in social life contained in *Centesimus Annus*. John Paul also writes about the threat of religious fundamentalism, which turns religious truth into ideology and a system of social solutions. But there were occasions in history when Christianity was itself reduced to an ideology.

It is really only in this context that we can understand the Pope's teaching on freedom. If freedom is not directed towards the truth, it amounts to nothing more than self-will, the possibility of doing whatever anyone happens to desire. If absolute truth is denied, then the supreme criterion in the life of any person becomes his own mind and conscience, which have the power to decide for themselves about the content of moral norms. The criteria of good and evil, or normal and abnormal, accepted by society become merely statistical. This accounts for the important stress in *Veritatis Splendor* on the fact that intrinsically evil acts exist.

The Pope argues vigorously that only truth gives sense and

meaning to human freedom; and because of this, human beings have an inner duty to search for truth and shape their lives according to its demands through development of the intellect and formation of the conscience. Preparing and taking responsibility for one's decisions is the real task in human life.

In this way, John Paul II strongly emphasizes the teaching of the Second Vatican Council. Despite appearances, this approach is not rigorism. For what is hidden behind it is, rather, a kind of optimism about human potential, faith in the capacity of men and women to recognize absolute truth and its moral possibilities, and to live according to these criteria.

The Pope's vision thereby becomes a defence of freedom. Man, a composite entity of body and spirit submerged in politics and culture, is not the slave of any power or structure, whether biological or psychological, economic, political or cultural. Yet this is sometimes a very difficult freedom. The Greek word *martyrein* means both testimony—which can be given only by those who are free—and martyrdom at the same time.

This is why *Veritatis Splendor* contains a section dedicated to the "theology of martyrdom". And it is why the Church, conscious that loyalty to the truth often demands heroism, does not impose truth but rather proposes it to human beings. The Pope writes in his 1990 encyclical on mission, *Redemptoris Missio*, that "the Church imposes nothing, she only proposes". In his 1981 apostolic exhortation, *Familiaris Consortio*, to which he refers in *Veritatis Splendor* 95, he had noted that "the Church interprets the moral norm and proposes it to all people of good will, without concealing its demands of radical perfection". And all people of good will give an answer within the totality of their freedom.

Reading the two encyclicals together, we see how they mutually complement each other. In *Veritatis Splendor*, the individual perspective predominates: the perspective of the human person, who is the subject of moral decisions. But *Centesimus Annus* discusses social life and the people who together create the economy, political life and culture.

One might say that in *Centesimus Annus* the horizontal dimension predominates. The Pope writes in a modern way about economics and politics, and about current threats to the natural and human environment. There are proportionately few references to Scripture, or to strict theological arguments. Indeed, the basic, almost sole, sources quoted are previous encyclicals of popes from Leo XIII to John Paul II himself.

By contrast, *Veritatis Splendor* moves in the vertical dimension, and the text deals with the contemporary scene only when speaking about evident threats to the truth. The encyclical is a great compendium of tradition, whose entire construction is founded on reflections on texts from Scripture. In no other encyclical does John Paul II make so many references to church writers and fathers, as well as the great medieval theologians. There are references to the councils of Vienna and Trent, and to the First and Second Vatican Councils. And there are quotations from Cardinal Newman, and from Popes Leo XIII, Pius XII and Paul VI.

But besides this rich variety of sources, the Pope also draws on the Church's early tradition and the Second Vatican Council. Among 184 footnotes, 58 refer to Christian antiquity and the Middle Ages (especially to St Augustine and St Thomas Aquinas) and 58 to the Second Vatican Council, where the encyclical gives absolute primacy to the pastoral constitution on the Church in the modern world, *Gaudium et Spes*. John Paul also refers to the new *Catechism of the Catholic Church*, the Code of Canon Law, the Missal, and documents of the Congregation for Catholic Education and the Congregation for the Doctrine of the Faith. We can boldly affirm that this latest encyclical attempts to sum up the Church's tradition as a whole in the light of Vatican II.

I have shown, then, how the "horizontal" *Centesimus Annus* and "vertical" *Veritatis Splendor* have pointed us towards a synthesis of John Paul II's fifteen years of teaching. These two very different documents are connected not only by the dialectic of truth and freedom, but also by John Paul's deep conviction that the splendour of God's truth can inspire societies and nations, and can illuminate the life of every person in our complex and tragic century.

A summons to reality

Oliver O'Donovan

No, it is not possible to read the encyclical from the middle out, as though the polemics were the meat of the matter and the rest all pious gravy. That would overlook the great care with which the controversies have been situated. Mapping the terrain of Christian moral concepts to show the context in which differences arise—that is the work the Pope has undertaken in the first of his three chapters, and, despite its easy homiletic style, nothing in it can simply be taken for granted. Here John Paul sketches the contours of moral theology as a whole, proving as he does so his relation to the aspirations of the Second Vatican Council a quarter-century ago. Moral theology, he tells us, is a pastoral and evangelistic response to the existential question constantly thrown up by the human agent who needs to find a ground and end of action.

This response unfolds in a carefully ordered sequence of forms. It is teleological; it offers a conception of the good. It is deontological, proposing a code of moral commands. It is eschatological, arousing a hope of transcendent perfection.

The order in which these three forms of response are presented is eloquent. The commands, the imperative elements of Christian ethics, both follow from and lead to visions of the good: at the beginning the good of God himself, at the end the good of human completion in God. This conceptual structure is then required to ground three aspects of the moral life: it is a following of Christ, it is empowerment by the Holy Spirit, it is a community tradition. All of which is meant to put discussions of natural law (quite literally) in their place.

Everyone has had a nice word to say about this first section. Not everyone has appreciated its innovative strength as a programme for moral theology. Future generations may find the splendour of *Veritatis Splendor* here in these pages which shape the moral discourse of the Church as an evangelical proclamation.

The third chapter, too, is something more than a sermon. It contains a doctrine of mission, which characterizes Christian moral witness as an acted proclamation of the cross. There is a striking emphasis on the potential conflict between faith and the totalizing social system of modern civilization. Protestants bred in the critical dialectical conceptions of Church and society from Barth to Hauerwas are likely to find this part of the encyclical, with its patristic sense of crisis, much closer to them than the bland Thomistic approach to cultural synthesis which used to be the hallmark of Vatican statements. Hauerwas himself, in his response to the encyclical in *Commonweal*, seized joyfully on the passage which makes martyrdom the primary paradigm of free witness. A different stream of Protestantism, aligned more closely with the World Council of Churches, may find the secondary paradigm, service of society, more congenial. The chapter is given a marked Augustinian flavour by a section in which the forgiveness of sins is seen as an essential condition of the Church's righteousness. This move, which suggests that the Vatican's positive reception for the Anglican-Roman Catholic International Commission's "Salvation and the Church" document was more than a flash in the pan, is a moment of sympathetic resonance for which few Protestants will have dared to hope.

Yet there is little sign that all this good news for Protestant Christians sprang from a self-conscious ecumenical agenda; and perhaps it makes the good news better if the convergences are spontaneous and unforced. Nor can I detect any conscious intent to respond to the challenges of liberation theology. But clearly the Pope is ready, in squaring up to the more dehumanizing determinants of Northern civilization, to learn from that source and to imitate the spirit of Christians who have confronted oppressive structures in the South.

In order to recover the critical edge in the Church's engagement with society, the Pope has undertaken a review of trends in formal ethical theory—an unexpected but by no means unpersuasive strategy. His thesis is the necessity of truth as the condition of freedom. Objectivity humbles tyrants. Totalitarianism is the child of moral scepticism, having cast itself loose from the critical authority that can challenge social structures. The prospect of an alliance between democratic civilization and moral relativism fills John Paul with alarm at its inevitably tyrannous tendency. A theory which supposes freedom in a vacuum, anterior to truth, a freedom to "create" moral values and "invent" right and wrong, has to be resisted in the name of evangelical freedom—which is the only freedom that can prove itself as a liberating social force.

This is the ground over which the Pope has elected to fight—not the traditional terrain of Catholic moral theology, by any means; but the decision indicates a cool assessment of trends in twentieth-century moral reasoning. On this chosen ground the encyclical is at home. Its maladroit moments come when it leaves it to pursue more traditional scholastic exercises.

The campaign is an ambitious one. It comprises four major critiques: one is directed against views which polarize freedom and nature, a second against over-subjective accounts of conscience, a third against an absolutizing of the "fundamental option" which can set it loose from the actual decisions people make, and the fourth attacks varieties of consequentialism. The positions under attack are rather disparate. Some stress the innovative powers of human resolve and will to mould and shape reality. Others are romantic, finding the essence of truth wrapped up within the self-conscious soul. Others again are rationalist, reducing all moral wisdom to varieties of calculative prudence.

What connects them all is a failure to provide a developed

account of the *field* of moral action, that is to say, of the created world with all its infinite variety of created goods and ends, into which any act that we design has to be projected, within which any act has to be justified. The view of human action common to these theories, one might say, is like that which one would find in the Book of Job if it were shorn of God's final speeches. The world appears as an empty stage for human merit to parade on, formless, undetermined, infinitely plastic, like the universe before God's first creative word. Action, in consequence, is shaped to the service of the agent-mind or agent-will, rather than to the service of the world. It loses its world-determined meaning *as* action—so that in some theories it comes to look like an expressive gesture revealing the secrets of the heart, in others like an instrumental technique manipulating the world to some end, and in still others virtually irrelevant to moral evaluation. The underlying connexion is the paradoxically "unworldly" character (in this specialist sense) of twentieth-century ethics: that is, its tendency to refuse the world that is given it in favour of some other world which it invents. This could be drawn out with patient exposition, but a public document, even a long one such as this encyclical, does not have infinite space for exposition at its command, and, not surprisingly, *Veritatis Splendor* sometimes gives the impression of having just one answer for every question.

That answer is true, forceful and to the point. Yet there is still room for a passing doubt as to whether the Pope has positioned himself in the best possible way to make it. He himself speaks out of a species of Christian idealism, which understands the rationality of moral law as something grounded in the human mind. He offers, indeed, some startling hostages to the claims of unaided natural reason. Is he himself sufficiently distant from the radical subjectivity on which he has set his sights? What is lacking in contemporary trends in moral thought is a sense of moral order in the world. Can he repair this with a stress on moral order in the mind? I am not sure. Perhaps there is some advantage, after all, in drawing the line against the extremities of idealism from within the idealist tradition. Even if the line is not drawn so cleanly, it safeguards the possibility of a true alliance between Christianity and idealism and avoids rejecting the wheat with the tares.

If there are any tares, that is. Some Catholic respondents have been quick to say that within the Catholic Church no one affirms what John Paul wishes to deny. (A response not strengthened by the afterthought, "And he got us all wrong anyway", like someone trying to escape through two doors simultaneously.) If it should prove to be so, nothing more serious is implied than that the Pope has a clearer view of wider intellectual trends than he has of what Catholic theologians are up to. The attempt to define where Christian moral theory has to take issue with sceptical alternatives is still a helpful one. But he thinks some theologians have been swayed, at least, by these trends, and I would judge he is right. No one is named, and he is not unappreciative of truths that may have helped to lead them in that direction. If it is a misunderstanding, no harm has been done and some good. We can all learn from misunderstandings that careful readers form of our positions.

Still, it is pardonable if, after more than a decade of bruising civil strife within their Church over moral issues, Roman Catholic respondents tend to read the encyclical as a manoeuvre in what they perceive as the Vatican's wider strategy. In this reading quite a formidable weight is attached to the final couple of pages about theologians and the teaching authority. Non-Catholic theologians like myself cannot judge these contextual perceptions with any insight, and we should not presume to parrot them. We are forced to read the text quite straightforwardly *as* text. But there is some value to be got, perhaps, from our innocent reactions, if only that of helping Roman Catholic colleagues sort out just where it is their problems lie. So far as I can see, they cannot lie in what is said about moral theory. Of course, an Anglican moral theologian does not expect to agree with what the Vatican says about the teaching authority; but I cannot find anything significantly new to choke on here.

And (dare I add?) the meaning of this document for the family quarrel may be much less important than what it offers the universal Church. By going behind particular issues to focus on the instrumentality and plasticity of modern moral reason, the Pope has gone to the heart of a philosophical situation in which all Christians now find themselves. If there is a place for a Petrine office in the Church (a matter on which I keep an open mind), surely this encyclical is a creditable example of the kind of service it may render.

A message in season

Mary Tuck

The fact that the Pope is a Pole is sometimes, in the secular press, held against him. He is presented as an old man, rigid, inflexible, from a culture that has learned a necessary harshness in the struggle against Communism. How can such a man speak to the liberal Western world?

His encyclical *Veritatis Splendor* has been presented by the secular press in much the same way; as a "Polish" encyclical, harsh, unyielding, restating moral and sexual rules of behaviour at their most stringent.

Curious to see for myself, I went out and (with some difficulty) bought a copy. At first sight it looks pretty defeating. Every page is scattered with footnotes, italics, quotations, references. Typography and production are not exactly reader-friendly.

But I persevered. And I think many should do so. I am not a moral theologian. I am an ordinary lay Catholic. But I read the encyclical straight through and found it accessible, clearly argued and poetic.

Its central message is about the reality of good and evil; the existence of absolute moral criteria. Some actions, the Pope insists, are wrong of their very nature. No matter how good the intention of the man who does them, such acts are forbidden and no good can come of them. This is a message foreign to our relativist culture. Utilitarian morality is pervasive. In considering any political topic—divorce law, the prison population, single parents—the public debate is almost always driven by considerations of social engineering. What would be the ends of our action? Would they contribute to the greatest good of the greatest number?

Many questions of social action may rightly be decided on such grounds. In Britain the available means of action are still constrained by some vague general sense that certain means of action are just "wrong"; not allowable. So the decision is usually to take the most prudent step within some unstated but real moral limits.

But if you come from a culture where within living memory it has been thought allowable to send whole populations to Siberia for the greatest good of the greatest number, then the need for some absolute limits to what is done must be more salient.

So it is the Polish Pope who has had to remind us that intention is not a sufficient guarantee of good action. His culture had felt on the bone the need for the protection of absolute moral law. Nor is this experience irrelevant to the Western democracies. The Pope rightly fears the "risk of an alliance between democracy and ethical relativism which would remove any sure moral reference-point from political and social life and on a deeper level make the acknowledgement of truth impossible" (101). Who can say this is not a real risk?

The Pope's message is a noble one but not without its difficulties. Readers of this book will already have some idea of what these are. They are most strongly present in the long second chapter of the encyclical where he tries to establish his position by arguing against various current schools of moral theology. This chapter is best read, as it comes in the encyclical, after the beautiful and inspiring first chapter, a meditation on the dialogue of Jesus with the rich young man, related in the nineteenth chapter of Saint Matthew's gospel.

Here the answers to the question "What good must I do?" are firmly set within the framework of biblical revelation. To the believing Christian this chapter is moving and deeply convincing. It shows the continuity of the old and new law; the way in which Jesus taught us to move from the observation of the commandments through to an acceptance of the divine invitation to "Come, follow me" and to the new life of grace which gives the power to "do what is true". This chapter can speak to those who find moral theology or abstract discussion arid. It is accessible to any biblical Christian. It is a great sermon.

The second, more argumentative chapter has a cooler, less poetic tone. The Pope proceeds by considering what he sees as errors in the teachings of various modern schools of moral theology. And since these schools have arisen in an attempt to make sense to the modern mind of ancient teachings, it is in this chapter that the modern reader, however predisposed to assent, will find difficulties.

For myself I must admit that I find the discussion of the nature of "intrinsically evil acts" (80) and the relative role in defining them of "intention" and the "object" of the act, to be more rather than less difficult than the treatment of the same subject by St Thomas. For instance, the Pope quotes St Thomas I-II.100.1 in support of the position that "the commandments contain the whole natural law" (79) and the teaching that certain acts are "intrinsically evil, always and *per se*" (80). But reference back to the *Summa Theologiae* (McDermott's translation; p. 299) shows that St Thomas adds at 100.8: "The ten commandments are unalterably right about what is just, but what can alter are the criteria which decide in particular cases whether this or that is murder or adultery or theft." Precisely. To admit this is not to slide into relativism. Thomas even adds boldly: "Sometimes the alteration is subject to human jurisdiction. In such matters, though not in all, men represent God."

Murder is wrong and we need to hold firmly to this truth. But the definition of murder though clear in essence is not always clear in particular cases. For instance, many women suspect that the Church has been more effective (even "liberal") in drawing distinctions concerning the exact nature of murder in matters of traditionally male interest such as war and justice, than it had in drawing distinctions in matters concerning sexual morality, marriage and motherhood.

The details of the moral argument will continue. But the Pope has pointed to the core issue. Whatever formulations we find, we must hold hard to the ancient truth that some things are wrong of their very nature. The glorious tradition of the old and the new law can lead us into the love and freedom of Christ. Both this freedom and this law are needed if society is to flourish.

But what of the vexed question of contraception? It is no secret, but a well attested fact, that few Western Catholics are convinced that contraception is always in conflict with the natural law. Indeed, very many are convinced that it is not. To include contraception in any list of things known, through revelation, tradition and the common consent of mankind, to be evil "of their very nature" would, for most Western Catholics, have shed doubt on the whole argument of the encyclical. It would have risked reducing the concept of natural law and the authority of the universal Church to the level of the arbitrary rulings of those sects who insist, on somewhat similar grounds, that blood transfusions are against nature.

Providentially (and I mean providentially) the encyclical seems to avoid, though only just, any unambiguous statement that contraception is intrinsically evil. The key paragraph is no. 80. Contraception is not included in the list of such acts quoted from Vatican II's pastoral constitution on the·Church in the modern world, *Gaudium et Spes*, in the first part of the paragraph. So far so good. But paragraph 80 ends with one continuous sentence, partly a quotation from Paul VI's *Humanae Vitae*, which runs: "With regard to contraceptive acts, and in reference to contraceptive practices . . . Pope Paul VI teaches '. . . It is never lawful to do evil that good may come of it—in other words, to intend directly something which of its very nature contradicts the moral order . . . even though the intention is to protect or promote the welfare of an individual, of a family or of society in general'."

The drafting is complex; but I believe just acceptable. We can all accept the teaching of Paul VI as quoted. It is a restatement of the central message of *Veritatis Splendor*. We can all accept that it needs to be borne in mind "with regard to" and "in reference to" contraceptive acts. But so considering, in great seriousness, most people do not believe that contraception is intrinsically evil.

So for the moment the danger of any unambiguous statement that contraception is intrinsically evil is just, if only just, avoided. But we must trust in Providence that the Holy Spirit will continue so to guide the Church that our pastors will continue to draw back, whatever their personal opinions, from extending the list of things which are intrinsically evil to a point which would damage those very concepts of absolute morality which the Church is so anxious to promulgate and which the world so needs.

The encyclical does not shirk the difficulties of living out its vision. Following on from the argument of chapter 2, chapter 3, "Lest the Cross of Christ be emptied of its power", reminds us that fidelity to truth and to goodness may sometimes require of us sacrifice; sacrifice *usque ad mortem*, even to the death of martyrdom. Once again the sombre experiences of the twentieth century shine through. Perhaps we needed the Polish Pope to write these words; far indeed from the cosy banalities of Western happy-clappy social Christianity.

"Doing good" may require heroic virtue. Fidelity to the law may need to be witnessed by death "so that the splendour of moral truth may be undimmed in the behaviour and thinking of individuals and society . . .. This witness makes an extraordinarily valuable contribution to warding off in civil society . . . a headlong plunge into the most dangerous crisis which can afflict man: the confusion between good and evil" (93). One feels Solzhenitsyn would applaud these words. They sum up the courage which the twentieth century has so often called for in the believer.

Perhaps for the sake of balance, there could have been more of a reminder in this section of the love of Christ; that the Christian call to courage and self-sacrifice can co-exist with the knowledge that the Church is composed of sinners. No Pope could wish Christ's Church to be confined to those with heroic virtue. But I suspect that priests underestimate just what heroism it takes to be a Catholic anyway and what constant daily heroism is practised by the ordinary people in the pew. They can meet the challenge, so long as they are not asked to observe rules they think are mistaken.

The latter part of the third chapter of the encyclical seems to have caused most anxiety among professional moral theologians. In it the Pope calls on the bishops to ensure "the reaffirmation of the universality and immutability of the moral commandments . . . particularly those which prohibit intrinsically evil acts" (115). It is impossible to have read the encyclical so far without feeling that he is right, and is addressing a problem of crucial and tragic centrality for human history. But does his clarion call mean that all debate must cease? Surely not. The fact that the important chapter 2 is itself couched in terms of argument shows that the Pope recognizes the exercise of reason in the light of revelation, to be, as always, the way forward.

Taken as a whole, this is an inspired encyclical with much to teach. Our intellectual life is bedevilled on all sides by relativity. There is the relativity of structuralist theory in literary academies, which stresses so strongly the possibility of variant readings of texts that the young are no longer able to read old books for profit. There is the relativity of certain schools of social scientists who would deny even to the findings of science any necessary connections with the real world. There is the relativity of secular moralists and politicians who regard as naïve any attempt to act according to what is right.

Our society may still be constrained by some vague notions of morality. No Western government could gain assent to policies so clearly wicked as making foreigners wear yellow stars or killing off the mentally ill. But are we confident this moral sense is not sliding? In my own specialist area of criminology, are we confident that the current British Government's policy of overcrowding our prisons is truly based on principles of morality and justice?

The encyclical can speak to secular constituencies only through the educated laity. I was left reflecting at the end of my reading that professional moral theologians may in some ways be its worst audience. They will inevitably read it with anxiety, because, as we have seen in this book, they will need to engage in detail with the Pope's arguments about particular schools of moral theology, some of which he may have unwittingly misrepresented or misunderstood in points of detail or of emphasis. Out of debate more clarity will come. But this anxiety perhaps blinds a little to the vision of the encyclical; a vision which those of us who live more fully in the secular world can see is both refreshing and inspiring.

It is an old vision, not a new one. But it needed to be preached and the Pope had preached it with eloquence and power. Some have queried the need. What, they ask, would be at all different in our society if the Pope's message were heard and accepted? Surely the experience of the Polish Pope gives the answer? When Solzhenitsyn left Russia he said that all that was necessary for the regime to fall was that its people would learn never to lie, but always to tell the truth. It was the *splendor veritatis* that bought down the Communist empire.

Who is to say what would happen to Western culture if we too could learn to walk in the light? I hope the message of the encyclical is heard and preached in schools and parishes. Too much Catholic education and preaching leaves the impression that all that is necessary to serve God is some vague sense of community and a readiness to give alms and support to the Third World. These things are necessary and need to be preached. But they do not fire the young with enough enthusiasm. Too many, bored, drift away. The more sombre ancient vision of the Pope, and its call to walk with God in heroic sanctity, may have more drama and more power.

I believe many are hungry for the core message of the encyclical. The only thing which would damage its acceptance would be if the lines of morality were drawn too wide, to include acts which the people of God (and many of their pastors) cannot see as evil. We must pray that does not happen. And we must look to the moral theologians, such as those who have contributed to this book, to help us.

9

Accent on the masculine

Lisa Sowle Cahill

To be a feminist is to be committed to the equality of women and men, and to cultivate a special sensitivity to the way women have been marginalised in the world's cultures and religions. Christian feminists draw on liberating strands within Christianity itself, especially in Scripture. Many have noted, for instance, that the creation stories present an original equality distorted by sin, that Jesus interacted with women in novel and affirmative ways, and that he made their roles in the religious community dependent on personal faith rather than on marital and maternal status.

In addition, Catholic Christian feminists both revise and renew the "natural law" approach so strongly developed within their tradition. Natural law moral thinking, rooted in Aquinas and visible in different ways in sexual teaching, bioethics, just war theory, and the social encyclicals, works from reasonable and critical generalisations on shared human experience. It is confident that moral common ground can be established among people with different cultural and religious traditions. The Catholic tradition has never stood for a narrow, sectarian morality, but has based its moral conclusions on an interpretation of human well-being in general. Thus, according to John Paul II's encyclical *Veritatis Splendor* "the natural law involves universality", is "inscribed in the rational nature of the person", and "makes itself felt to all beings endowed with reason and living in history" (51). Objectivity in matters of morality and justice was highlighted by the Pope himself, when interpreting the encyclical to a group of bishops from the United States in Rome.

Many Catholic feminists supplement a liberating reading of biblical texts with an appeal to women's experience as disclosing the "full humanity" and equality of women and men (in the phrase of Rosemary Radford Ruether). Pointing out that interpretation of the natural law has always been undertaken through specific historical and cultural perspectives, they argue that patriarchal definitions of human sexual nature and gender roles are distorted rather than built on what human experience demands. For instance, the fulfilment of human sexuality is through mutual love, not primarily through procreation; parenthood is as important a role for men as for women; and both sexes make contributions to the common good through public as well as domestic vocations.

Feminist critics frequently call attention to women's actual experience in order to challenge "universals" which, they claim, reflect the biases of those in power. Women's experience may not tally with female nature and roles as prescribed, especially when cultural and historical variations are taken into account. Feminists, in turning to the testimony of experience, often follow philosophers like Derrida and Foucault, who mistrust any appeal to an impartial rationality which can issue universal moral dicta. North American and European women zestfully dismantle culture-bound gender stereotypes by celebrating the "difference" and uniqueness of previously excluded voices. Feminists may rightly claim that many traditional Christian depictions of their natural or divinely mandated roles do not correspond to the reality and value of women's own lives.

Yet one problem that arises as a result of feminist theology's appeal to "experience" is the danger of replacing oppressive generalisations with bottomless particularity. If women's experience alone is exalted as the final moral standard, we run the danger of a feminist relativism which is ultimately unable to give any real reasons for preferring equality rather than hierarchy.

It is important to move back from particularity to the sense of shared human values which is so central to natural law. Women and men suffering economic and political repression, as well as sexism, appeal to values—justice, rights, and duties—which can be seen to hold true across eras, cultures, religions. *Veritatis Splendor*, then, may serve as a resource for feminist theology and ethics by affirming a moral foundation on the basis of which injustice of all kinds can be recognised and eradicated.

The question feminists will bring to this encyclical, however, is whether its defence of moral objectivity is not fatally wounded by a too visible male point of view, and by a tendency to resolve genuinely difficult questions by resort to authority. Although documents of the teaching authority are never notable for inclusive language, this encyclical accentuates patriarchal language and traditional gender imagery to a remarkable degree when contrasted even with papal writings such as *Familiaris Consortio* (the apostolic exhortion "On the Family" of 1981) and *Mulieris Dignitatem* (the apostolic letter "On the Dignity and Vocation of Women" of 1988). While both the latter still portray women's nature in maternal terms, *Familiaris Consortio* explicitly affirms greater social access for women (23), and *Mulieris Dignitatem* holds up Mary Magdalene as a leader and "apostle to the Apostles" (16). It thus comes as a disappointment that in *Veritatis Splendor* objective human morality—the encyclical's central theme — is relentlessly advocated as necessary to "man's" good.

Veritatis Splendor reasserts traditional sexual norms, which have in the past been tied to the role of women as wives and mothers. It makes no attempt to incorporate any special references to women's good, women's experience, or vocations of women beyond domesticity in its treatment of sexual norms which have a special impact on women (such as the ban on contraception). It condemns rape and prostitution, which have always been seen as sexual sins, yet does not specifically condemn sexual violence as a crime against women, nor social oppression of women.

Three important areas in which a feminist point of view will occasion criticism as well as appropriation of *Veritatis Splendor* are the body, intrinsically evil acts, and gender roles.

The moral meaning of the human body is both controversial and important across a number of issues today, many of which are central in Catholic teaching and for feminists. How does human (sexual) nature as embodied and physical relate to human nature as rational and free? When and how may freedom legitimately control the body in order to achieve "higher" human ends? In condemning artificial birth control, the teaching authority attaches great value to the physical structure of sexual acts as demanding an "openness" to procreation. On the other side, many feminists insist that women's self-determination requires them to be able to control their own reproductive powers.

A related issue is the development of reproductive technologies, which range from enhancing the conceptive potential of intercourse to *in vitro* fertilisation and the use of donor gametes. What is the importance of physical relationships, both sexual and genetic, in evaluating the acceptability of these methods? Should the conception of a child be accomplished always and only through a sexual act, and never in a laboratory setting which compensates for infertility? Would conception by artificial insemination or *in vitro* fertilisation be acceptable if the spouses provided the ova and sperm, enabling both to share a genetic relation to the child, and conferring on their marriage the fertility lacking to their individual sexual acts? To what degree does or should the body establish moral values, or limit the means we may use in removing obstacles to the realisation of personal and social values we recognise as important?

Veritatis Splendor resists the idea that the body is simply freedom's "raw material" (46), and proposes that reason, freedom, soul, and body are linked in a unity (48, 50). This is an important corrective of some liberal feminisms which tend, at least theoretically, to make choice a moral absolute. Many feminists want to recover the integrity and worth of women's bodies over against patriarchal control, yet find it difficult to show exactly how embodiment functions as a positive moral value if it can never set limits on free choices. A profound affirmation of women's full moral agency requires more than the simplistic promotion of free choice, as most Catholic feminists recognise.

Yet the linkage which the encyclical makes of reason, freedom, soul and body leaves unresolved the critical question of whether the elements in this unity are all of equal importance. Church teaching holds that "love" is a foundational meaning of sex, but tends to revert to a sacralisation of physical processes whenever sex is the moral issue. The precise value of the body and of bodily relationships in setting parameters for freedom needs better analysis from both a natural law and a feminist perspective. Catholic teaching will remain unable to address these issues effectively as long as it is perceived as raising them only in order to reassert sexual norms which had their origin in the primacy of procreation and in women's subordination to men through their procreative role.

What then, secondly, has a feminist to say about a central proposition of the encyclical, that there are in principle "intrinsically evil acts", which in themselves and apart from any circumstances and intentions are objectively sinful? The philosophical objections to this formulation are numerous and complex. From a feminist perspective, we may note two points.

First, traditional instances of intrinsic evil have higher visibility in the sexual category than in any other. Yet in the present encyclical masturbation, fornication, contraception, homosexuality, and abortion come in for mention only a couple of times (47, 80). This is certainly good in that it puts sexuality in perspective as one among other areas of moral concern. But it creates an ambiguous situation, in which traditional sexual norms can be played up or down as central to the meaning of the encyclical. Feminist sympathy for its message will obviously be higher if the encyclical can encourage creative reflection on the moral value of the body, rather than if it is used to shore up definitions of women's identity and roles that are based on the procreative function.

Secondly, the encyclical itself obfuscates the concept of intrinsically evil acts by giving examples on disparate levels, which are for the most part not under dispute by the so-called "proportionalists" it opposes (6, 80). Murder, adultery, stealing, genocide, torture, prostitution, slavery, "subhuman living conditions", "arbitrary imprisonment" and "degrading conditions of work" have few if any defenders among Catholic theologians. The point of course is that these terms and phrases do not, as the encyclical implies, define acts in the abstract, but acts (like intercourse or homicide) *together with the conditions or circumstances* in which they become immoral. Such acts are indeed wrong, because immoral circumstances have already been specified in the examples given. A single term like "murder" or "genocide" makes it clear that what might have been a justifiable "act in itself" (homicide) was done in wrong circumstances; or a phrase like "killing an innocent person", which spells out exactly what circumstances of homicide are meant, results in an absolute moral norm. About this there is little disagreement.

Is it really so easy to speak of "acts in themselves" as the defenders of that category and the opponents of it alike suggest? A key contribution of feminism is to highlight the social context of moral agency, and to be attentive to concrete human relationships. Upon reflection, it is evident that even an "act" like contraception is really intercourse-in-the-circumstances-of-birth-avoidance (by "artificial" means). Indeed, intercourse as the so-called "act" at the centre of sexual debates could itself be broken down into male (or female) sexual response and perfomance, to be set "circumstantially" in a heterosexual or homosexual context. Where does "act" end and "circumstance" begin?

Feminist moral theologians, among others, might be led to conclude that when we speak of acts, we focus attention on a nexus of practical, physical, causal, and moral relationships, but do not mark off absolute boundaries around a moral event. Hence the whole discussion of the moral neutrality or evil of sexual acts in the abstract may depend on a category which a more relational philosophical approach reveals to be questionable. Perhaps the lesson to be learned is that we reject some decisions and practices as morally abhorrent not on the basis of properties they possess "in themselves" and apart from the dispositions and circumstances of agents, but because of their concrete and practical degradation of the human persons involved. Moral evil will not be recognised as such simply because an "intrinsic evil" flag is waved over it;

substantive and reasonable arguments must be advanced about the specific nature of the acts in question.

The third area where a feminist approach has a special contribution to make concerns gender roles. Especially in Western, industrialised nations, women's and men's roles are fast changing. The suitability of women's gifts for public contributions to the common good is increasingly recognised, while men find rewards in family life and child-rearing. *Veritatis Splendor*'s neglect of these developments in the understanding of masculine and feminine nature casts a dark shadow over the Church's authority to specify truly the human goods of sex, gender and family.

Most problematic is the sexist language in which "man's" nature is defined. The opening line sets the tone: "The splendour of truth shines forth in all the works of the Creator and, in a special way, in man, created in the image and likeness of God." Exclusive language applied to a biblical text which explicitly associates both male and female with the divine image is unnecessary and even embarrassing. Five years earlier, *Mulieris Dignitatem* spoke of "the creation of the human being as male and female, made in the image and likeness of God" (11). How can we with any credibility make the case to a pluralistic (and confused) culture that the Catholic tradition has valid insights about sex, commitment, love and parenthood, when the most current official documents retrieve a male-oriented perspective as a prelude to asserting the Church's prerogative to interpret the Gospel and human nature?

The conclusion of the encyclical comes full circle with its eulogy of Mary as "Mother of Mercy". Following a 174-page promotion of negative moral norms, this section clearly was meant to encourage pastoral understanding of "human frailty and sin" (118). But gender stereotypes move into full view as Mary is exalted as the nurturing, loving and compassionate Mother of Jesus, a moral model for whom "freedom" meant "giving herself to God" and "accepting" God's will (120). "She understands sinful man and loves him with a Mother's love." Why not praise Jesus' compassion, forgiveness and obedience, while holding up Mary's courage and the leadership of other women like Mary Magdalene as contemporary models for both men and women?

From the perspective of a Catholic feminist moral theologian, *Veritatis Splendor* holds out promise for the reinforcement of our common moral foundations. Yet it also illustrates why those foundations must be laid more cautiously and critically, and why Catholic "natural law" ethics has been a particular target of feminist attack.

10

Manuals and rule books

Herbert McCabe

Several commentators have found the most difficult teaching of the encyclical *Veritatis Splendor* to be its insistence that we can describe certain kinds of human acts which will be morally wrong whenever and however and for whatever reason they are performed. If, the document claims, an action falls under such a description, we know it to be wrong regardless of anything else we might know about it. Such a description must, of course, be a human one: it cannot be merely an account of what physically happens; it must include reference to what the agent intends in his act (though not to any consequences he may intend). Unlike a number of Catholic moralists, I think there are good reasons for holding this position, though I do not find them in the encyclical. On the other hand, I do not think the doctrine has the central importance there accorded to it and therefore find the scarcely veiled threats to Catholic teachers who think differently quite out of place and distasteful.

If you want to play football well, you will, let us suppose, make use of two books. The first is written by an experienced coach and tells you what the good and bad moves are in the game and how to practise the former and avoid the latter. It aims to help you acquire certain football skills. Learning such skills does not consist in understanding and remembering what you have read in this training manual; for football is not a theoretical but a practical skill—it can only be learnt by long practice guided by the manual. In fact, as you become more skilled you will refer less and less to the manual. Moreover, if you become expert you may, on occasion, recognize that the really excellent move would involve doing just what, in the manual, you were told never to do. Thus the book provides for the learner a reliable but not infallible guide to playing good football.

Besides the training manual, however, you will also need another book: you will need the rule book. This will tell you, amongst other things, what moves count as fouls. A foul is a bad or forbidden move, but it is not playing football badly: it is not playing football at all, but pretending to. You will doubtless have reasons for making a foul move (you may want your team to retain its place in the league table, for example) but they are not, and could not be, reasons within a game of football. A team which because of a foul seems to win had not in fact won a game of football. Given that what you are playing is football, there are no circumstances in which to make a foul move could be legitimate. The rule book does not tell you anything about acquiring skills in football; it simply tells you the rules and the kinds of action that would break them. At crucial points it is essential to know what is fair play and what is foul; and this is a fairly simple matter of information. The mere spectator can know this just as well as the most expert player. The rule book defines the context within which we may become skilled players: it in no way helps us to do so.

I hope I have managed to make clear what I see as the distinction between manuals of instruction which provide generalizations about what to do and not to do in order to help you to acquire skills in a game, and rule books which tell you the laws of the game and what counts as breaking them (of course in the real world of games the situation is rather more complex). Readers might, in passing, like to know that in my edition of the *Summa Theologiae*, of the 1,496 pages devoted to what we now call "moral theology", St Thomas spends just 22 pages on law, of which seven are directly about natural law. All the rest is concerned in various ways with virtues and vices—though this includes 300 pages on the virtue of justice in which there are, from time to time, references to law.

Now it seems to me that the encyclical *Veritatis Splendor* is, in great part, an attack on those who want to read the rule book as though it were a training manual by those who want to read the manual as though it were a rule book. Neither seems to have adverted to the fact that they are logically quite different kinds of discourse. The rule book, for example, is about individual acts, whereas the manual is about how to acquire dispositions.

Bill Shankley, when manager of Liverpool, said, "Football is not a matter of life and death: it is far more important". I am not taking that particular splendid truth literally; I just think that clarity about one can help towards clarity about the other. The obvious difference is that football is a human artefact: it is we who decide what the game shall be. We write the rule book of its laws (though we do then have to discover by experience how best to play it—how to write the manual). Human life, on the other hand, is a natural phenomenon (or gift from God) which we did not invent; though much inventiveness as well as experience has to go into finding out how best to live it. Like a game, it is difficult and challenging, involves successful and unsuccessful play; and, like a game, it has boundaries, to transgress which means playing some other game which is not what human life is about; and these boundaries and transgressions can be set forth as rules. But human living demands, above all, skills transmitted through education, especially those called virtues: skills in doing all things as befits a good human being. Although we are born with certain instincts and tendencies, inherited from our prelinguistic ancestors, which are valuable to us but simply not adequate to the complexity of linguistic life and society, we are not born with virtues— though some people are born with tendencies which make it easier for them to acquire this or that virtue. But virtues have to be acquired by our learning from each other or the Holy Spirit or both.

It is, then, a significant difference that what football is (and thus what counts as a foul) can be changed by a decision of the FA, whereas we cannot decide, but only discover, what human life is (and what counts as a foul in it). It seems to me that the encyclical wastes a good deal of time making this point since it would be hard to find any Catholic moralists who do suppose (as Richard Hare and the early Existentialists used to) that human morality is exactly like football, a human artefact invented some time ago.

On a visit to the United States during the Vietnam war I got to know a group engaged in a clandestine activity of which the American government did not approve. They were smuggling those who conscientiously objected to killing people in what they rightly saw as an unjust war out of the United States to such refuges as Sweden. Within this group there were those who were very committed and hard-working and those who were less so. One heard grumbling about those who were not pulling their weight, not entirely to be relied on to write the necessary letters, attend the meetings or provide the promised transport . . . and so on. When, a year or so later, I returned to the States, I learnt that one of the apparently most enthusiastic members of the group had turned out to be a government agent who had shopped them all to the police, so that several were in prison.

There was clearly a difference not merely of degree but of kind between those inadequately dedicated because of carelessness, selfishness or laziness and the action of betraying the whole project. The former played the "game" badly, the latter was a move equivalent to a "foul". Thus Alasdair MacIntyre (in his book *After Virtue*) says: "Aristotle . . . recognises that his account of the virtues has to be supplemented by some account, even if a brief one, of those types of action which are absolutely prohibited." Aristotle's city state, the *polis*, had its basis in *philia* (a word perhaps not adequately translated by "friendship" in the modern sense: it is more like companionship with trust, a kind of *esprit de corps*). *Philia* does, of course, involve affection, but precisely the affection arising from solidarity in a shared important project (such as marriage), a solidarity which Aristotle regards as the precondition for justice itself. It is acts incompatible with this *philia* that are the ones absolutely ruled out.

St Thomas develops Aristotle in at least two ways. In the first place the biblical doctrine of God as Creator (a Jewish notion not available to Aristotle) enables him to extend the analysis of the good human life from the *polis* of citizens under the authority of those chosen to rule to the quasi-political community of human creatures under the universal authority of the Creator. (It is hard to find a reasonable basis for "human" rights—as distinct from the rights of citizens in this or that community—without this notion of a Creator with "universal jurisdiction".)

In the second place, St Thomas takes Aristotle's political notion of *philia* (*amicitia* in his language) as his model for the *caritas* which is the foundation of the community of the human family as, not merely creatures, but children of God. So (in I–II. 88) he distinguishes between, on the one hand, not living the life of the Spirit well, perhaps through neglecting the cultivation of the virtues through prayer (for these firm dispositions are not now simply acquired by education but are the gift of the Holy Spirit), and, on the other hand, acts which are just incompatible with membership of a community sustained and defined by *caritas*. Those acts which cut at the root of human community thereby cut at the roots of our community in *caritas*. It would seem, for example, that there could be no human community based on friendship in which the killing of the innocent was treated with indifference; and hence such an action is a rejection of solidarity with each other, and thus a departure from the shared divine life which is the gift of the Spirit.

Now, the question arises: how are we to identify those acts which are not merely inadequacies in living the life of *caritas* but actually incompatible with the *caritas* upon which human community depends? It is a mistake to think that we find the answer to this by looking at a list of wrongdoings and arranging them in order of "gravity". St Thomas's answer is: by the use of our practical reasoning and also by faith in divine revelation; and the deliveries of these two sometimes overlap. In its primary meaning, for him, "natural law" just is our capacity for practical reasoning; reasoning, that is, about what to do, based on the principle "seek good and avoid evil", just as theoretical reasoning about what to think is based on the principle "seek truth, do not contradict yourself".

Unlike the sub-linguistic creatures, we have a capacity to make decisions about our own lives, and this exercise of *prudentia* on our part he sees as a sharing in the exercise of *providentia* on God's part. There is, for St Thomas, no built-in code or "voice of conscience", no innate grasp of moral truths. We are, indeed, born with instinctive tendencies to action but these are the voice, not directly of God but of our animal ancestry; they are to be respected, not as a substitute for, but as a factor to be taken into account in, our rational decision about what to do. Practical reasoning is not thinking about what laws to have but about what, on a particular occasion, to do. (The conclusion of the "practical syllogism" is an action.) Laws prohibiting certain types of action arise through our practical reflection on our thinking: deciding that it does not have to go on any more, because this action (for example, the killing of an innocent person) already calls in question the whole context within which practical thinking takes place, much as treason calls in question the very society in which it operates (it is important that foreigners cannot commit treason).

In this matter, however, as in all others, the exercise of practical reasoning is fallible. St Thomas thought that we were not very likely to be good at practical reasoning: we are so subject to self-deception and shoddy thinking, as a consequence of original sin, that, in practice, we only grope uncertainly towards the right answers (the right actions). So it was kindly of God to reveal (at least to his chosen people) the ten commandments: not as principles from which practical thinking should start, but as markers of the boundary where it might as well stop. That is what I meant by saying that the deliveries of practical reason and of faith sometimes overlap. God reveals what we might have worked out for ourselves but "only after a long time and with the admixture of many errors". A corollary of this, however, is that although we may have been too scatterbrained to work it out for ourselves, we could, by hindsight, recognize that it is not unreasonable. To see this we must recognize that the commandments are limits rather than principles.

The commandments, says St Thomas, concern matters that are fairly obvious deliveries of practical reasoning. In theoretical reasoning we do not have to do much work to recognize certain obvious logical fallacies, and similarly in practical reasoning it is not too hard to see that the kinds of thing prohibited in the decalogue are reasonably prohibited. But when they have become not just reasonable to our fallible minds but precepts from the infinite intelligence of God, their *status* is changed. The very fact of their being revealed makes them part of God's mysterious friendship with us, part of his sharing of his life with us. So now murder, for example, is not only an act of defiance of the project of human living together, it is, at a deeper level, a spurning of God's friendship, a breach of *caritas* with God. So, for St Thomas, a direct contravention of the revealed precepts of the decalogue is a"mortal" sin because the life in the Spirit that it rejects can only be restored by a miracle equivalent to resurrection from the dead.

The encyclical (79) speaks of "the commandments, which, according to St Thomas (I–II.100.1), contain the whole natural law". This is quite untrue. What St Thomas proposes in this article is the altogether different teaching that all the moral precepts (of the Old Law) belong to the natural law. For him, the natural law, being nothing but the exercise of practical reasoning, concerns any and every kind of specifically human activity. Thus the use of artificial contraceptives, say, or homosexual acts or masturbation or *in vitro* fertilization, none of which are mentioned in the decalogue, come within the scope of natural law simply because we can reason practically about them. On the other hand, perhaps in their case, since they are not *revealed* to us as prohibited, we should be chary of speaking of "mortal sin" in their connection. Moreover it must, surely, remain an open question whether objections to these practices should really be seen as part of the absolute rule book and not rather part of the more flexible manual of instruction intended to guide us as we grow to maturity in the virtue of temperateness.

In general, I think it must be said that the encyclical makes a bad case for a good thesis: that we need absolute prohibitions as well as instruction in the paths of virtue. I think it fails because, despite its frequent references to St Thomas, it is still trapped in a post-Renaissance morality, in terms of law and conscience and free will. Amongst Christians this commonly shows itself in attempts to *base* an account of Christian morality on the ten commandments, and this can only lead to a sterile polarization of "legalism" or "liberalism". You cannot fit the virtues into a legal structure without reducing them to dispositions to follow the rules. You can, however, fit law and obedience to law into a comfortable, though minor, niche in the project of growing up in the rich and variegated life of virtue. It is a pity that a major attempt to restate Christian morality should not have tapped the resources of a more ancient Aristotelian tradition, such as St Thomas inherited and transformed, which sees human life as the movement towards our real selves and towards God guided by the New Law which, as he insists, is no written code but nothing other than the presence in us of the Holy Spirit.

Beyond the encyclical

John Finnis

Faith, not sex, is the theme of *Veritatis Splendor*. In this concluding chapter, I ask whether the encyclical adequately responds to the situation it identifies and to the crisis of faith (cf. 4, 5, 88) it addresses.

In suggesting that the encyclical is basically about sex, commentators have neglected many of the Pope's most important concerns. Human rights, for example. John Paul II makes clear that the contemporary dissenting moral theologians' attempted "adjustment" of the moral teachings of Catholic faith is incompatible with inviolable human rights.

He teaches: "Even though intentions may sometimes be good, and circumstances frequently difficult, civil authorities and particular individuals never have authority to violate the fundamental and inalienable rights of the human person. In the end, only a morality which acknowledges certain norms as valid always and for everyone, with no exception, can guarantee the ethical foundation of social co-existence . . ." (97).

For instance, nobody has an inviolable right to life unless there is an exceptionless moral norm: never choose to kill an innocent human being. (And if this right is not inviolable, none is.) If appropriate circumstances and good intentions can sometimes justify choosing to kill an innocent, the lives of each of us depend on *everyone* judging, at every moment, that in the circumstances no greater good would be achieved, or greater evil avoided, by killing us.

Many theologians, all over the world, fail to confront this implication of their position. They talk rather about semen-sampling, or "theft" in time of necessity (when sub-personal goods revert to their original status as common to all in need). They misrepresent the encyclical as little more than an elaborate attempt to bolster the Church's teaching on contraception. If they talk of killing, it is only to complain that the encyclical has overlooked the "exceptions" of capital punishment, just war, or self-defence.

They overlook the relevant exceptionless norm which the Church's tradition, authoritatively interpreting revelation, has constantly and most firmly taught as a truth to be held definitively by every Catholic: it is always wrong to choose to kill the innocent, whatever the circumstances. The truly inviolable right to life corresponds to that norm, whose exceptionlessness their attempted "adjustment" of the traditional moral teaching rejects.

Of course, theologians of this kind meant only to make a minor adjustment in order to deal with rare and very difficult cases. But once it is allowed that a "proportionate reason" can justify choosing to kill an innocent person, the genie is out of the bottle and exceptions cannot be contained. None of these theologians has ever explained how one can rationally tell when a reason is not, in their sense, proportionate. (The arguments showing that no such explanation is possible remain unanswered.) So anyone who has a reason for choosing to kill someone is liable to regard that reason as proportionate.

A theologian of this kind who happens to be on the scene may say: that's not what I call a proportionate reason. But if pressed, he (here an *inclusive* pronoun!) can produce no rational argument to show that it is not proportionate. Suppose he meets a hospital ethics committee who consider the great suffering of very ill

patients a proportionate reason for killing them. Perhaps he will
say this is not a proportionate reason for killing. Asked why not,
he may say that his conscience tells him the reason is not proportionate. But those with a reason to kill will reply that their
consciences tell them it is.

The theologian may respond: conscience should be guided by
the Church's tradition. But the response is empty, coming from
theologians who have already appealed to "proportionate reasons"
to make exceptions to the specific moral norms most constantly
and firmly taught in the course of that tradition. Proportionalism's
appeal to "proportionate reasons" identifiable neither by reason
nor by Catholic faith points everyone to decisions of "conscience"
grounded in whatever one *feels* appropriate, all things considered.

Dissenting theologians may well concede that licensing exceptions to the norm against contraception has resulted in Catholics
generally contracepting whenever they fell it appropriate. But,
they will say, that is indeed the true norm: contraception is
appropriate when ever you judge it appropriate for your marriage.
And meanwhile, Catholics have not taken to killing in the way
my argument suggests they are liable to.

But this line of defence fails. In advanced countries such as the
United States, approval by Catholics of abortion (and presumably
their resort to it) approximates to the general population's. Perhaps
dissenting theologians deplore this as much as the Pope (cf. 84).
But they should not be surprised by what their adjustment of
traditional moral teaching has wrought. Allowing exceptions and
justifying any choice to kill an innocent person radically transforms one's attitude towards human life as such. Making and
carrying out any choices (even if not to kill someone but only, for
instance, to condone someone else's getting an abortion) on the
basis of that transformed attitude reshapes individual character and
social practices.

Witness the record of non-believing humanism. This historical
movement set out with limited political concessions: to save the
country one may perhaps sacrifice—even choose to kill—an innocent. But it moved on, to the Leninist massacres ("no omelette
without breaking eggs"), the Allied terror-bombing belatedly
condemned by Vatican II, ever more widespread resort to

abortions of convenience, and the killing of defective children. Now euthanasia is resurgent, half a century after an embarrassed silence fell in 1945.

The first victims of such transformations of individual character and social practice are the weak. So the Pope puts the significance of the exceptionless moral norms like this: "When it is a matter of the moral norms prohibiting intrinsic evil, there are no privileges or exceptions for anyone. It makes no difference whether one is the master of the world or the 'poorest of the poor' on the face of the earth. Before the demands of morality we are all absolutely equal" (96).

Someone will object: many other cultures, such as ancient Greece and Rome, allowed the intentional killing of innocents in certain limited cases without this leading to mass murder. So, allowing exceptions to received Christian moral norms need pose no threat of boundless moral decadence.

Our culture, however, is different. Judaeo-Christian revelation annihilated all the strange gods, and with them everything beyond the human which channelled and restrained human desires. The natural world lost its old sacredness. The only holy reality remaining was the one God. Nothing else, apart from man, determined meanings and values which man could recognize and had to respect. As God's image, man shared in his dignity, and man's innate grasp upon the principles of right and wrong was confirmed as participation in God's wisdom and love. While the goods which fulfil human beings here below—life, knowledge, friendship—retained the value they always had, they took on a new value as anticipated ingredients of a far grander fulfilment in the heavenly kingdom.

From this world-view, subtract God. What remains? Man— but no longer in God's image. Man's natural grasp on the principles of right and wrong—but not as a participation in anything, since there is nothing beyond man in which those principles could be a participation. The value of the things which fulfil human beings—but only insofar as this value might satisfy this or that person's or group's desire.

But desires conflict. Are others' desires to decide what is to happen to me and to those I care about? Not if I can help it!

Unfortunately, however, everyone shares the same thought. All are anxious to avoid becoming others' pawns, and each requires others' help in achieving his or her personal goals. So, few dare *utter* what every clear-headed post-Christian humanist thinks: since the God of Moses and Jesus (and even of Socrates) does not exist, everything is permitted. Still, the shell of traditional morality remains valuable—indeed, indispensable—to shape the behaviour of those who might impede me and mine from satisfying our desires.

In short, for the post-Christian mind traditional moral norms are no longer objectively binding. Yet they are still accepted by many people as divinely given, and conformed to by many others out of cultural inertia. Indeed, the natural law remains written on post-Christian hearts (cf. Rom. 2:14–15), so that, to a considerable extent, contemporary non-believers still know, communicate and act on moral truth. Thus most people's lives are better than their theories, in matters on which individual desires and corrupt social practices do not blind them.

And, as I say, the clear-headed non-believer realizes that conformity to the traditional moral norms still accepted in one's society is generally necessary for social order and personal reputation, both of which are essential for achieving one's goals. The shell of traditional morality *seems* to house a genuinely humanistic spirit long after the soul has departed.

But morality robbed of its objectivity and made an instrument of human wilfulness is radically unstable (cf. 1, 99, 105, 106). Whenever fulfilment of desires seems to them worth the cost in social stability and repute, people will make exceptions for themselves. The first socially approved exception to a norm such as, one may never choose to kill an innocent person, shows that there is no reason why we should limit satisfying our desires provided we are willing to accept that cost or risk. For people in this situation, there is no true fidelity, no bond of community except mutual agreement while it lasts.

Post-Christian thinking now dominates the contemporary world. In affluent nations, the economy is the servant of desires, which it creates and offers to fulfil without limit. The media are servants of this economy, and those responsible for them find it in their own interest to promote post-Christian thinking. In some places, Marxist ideology provided something very similar in its deep reality though transposed in its more superficial features. Even those who still cling to Jewish or Christian faith are more and more infected, as the encyclical points out (88).

How have theologians responded? Many have done their very best to help the faithful feel comfortable in the "real" world. Thus, they have proposed helpful theories of autonomy, conscience, fundamental option, proportionalism and so on.

Veritatis Splendor rejects those theories as "incompatible with revealed truth" (29) and thus with Catholic faith. This *judgment* is to be found, not in the encyclical's sketches of the theories, but in the commentary on Jesus' dialogue with the rich young man (see 52, the last sentence) and the repeated use of Romans 3:8 and I Corinthians 6:9–10 to verify the teaching with which dissenting theories are incompatible (see 49, 78–81).

The encyclical's reaffirmation that there are intrinsically evil acts, exceptionless specific moral norms and inviolable human rights is philosophically defensible and manifestly necessary to preserve the moral substance of Christian faith. But, as is suggested by the way the Pope's long-meditated judgment was promptly rejected by leading theologians (and their followers), the encyclical's teaching hardly begins to reach to the bottom of the crisis afflicting the Church.

As the Pope makes plain to every honest and careful reader, that crisis concerns not contraception so much as the whole of sexual morality, not sexual morality as much as morality's very foundations, and not even the foundations of morality so much as God's revelation of himself and faith responding to that revelation. And this last and deepest issue the encyclical points to rather than tackles squarely.

Dissenting positions in contemporary moral theology, carefully considered, are implausible unless one presupposes a post-Enlightenment, rather than Catholic, conception of the Bible, and a theory of revelation which precludes the use of revelation as a standard for evaluating theological theories and contemporary "Christian" experience. Given those presuppositions, one can be a "believing" Catholic while conforming one's conscience to the world. No longer "slaves to righteousness", we are thus freed to live "according to the flesh".

So, beyond *Veritatis Splendor*—and of even greater priority than an eventual definitive magisterial judgment on the received teaching concerning intrinsically evil acts—the Church awaits a still more fundamental definitive judgment, by the Pope and the other bishops, on certain "reconceptions" of revelation and faith which are at least as widespread in Scripture scholarship and fundamental theology (and hence also in moral theology) as dissenting moral opinions are among moral theologians.

Definitions condemning those "reconceptions" as incompatible with Catholic faith would coerce nobody. Rather, such definitions would be a service to truth and conscience. For the consciences of believers they would clarify the bases of their belief. For the consciences of non-believers, and of those choosing unbelief, they would clarify what it is that is proposed to them for belief by the successors of the Apostles, charged with teaching all nations to observe all that Jesus commanded. Nor would such definitions divide the Church. Rather they would identify where the unity of the faith, and thus of Christ's Church, in truth resides.

Such definitions could also help the Church to respond to another basic element in the crisis: loss of Christian hope, and pastoral silence about the last things. Only robust faith in the revelation consummated in the life, death, resurrection and teachings of Jesus, and transmitted by the apostles, will sustain the hope for the heavenly kingdom and for some share in it. (And one cannot *hope* for something one regards as *inevitable, if it exists at all.*)

Between hope and morality there is a relation far deeper than any matter of incentives and deterrents. God's commandments—confirming what is accessible to practical reasonableness even without divine revelation—protect innocent human life and other fundamental goods of persons (13, 48, 50, 78, 79, 90). These are goods meant to last forever as elements in the divine-human communion for which God created humankind. Those who violate such elements of the everlasting kingdom refuse to make themselves ready for that kingdom. By God's gratuitously promised gift, those who respect those fundamental goods in every choice—as the tradition's exceptionless norms require—thereby build up the material of the kingdom, even when the bad consequences avoidable by, say, choosing instead to kill an innocent seem overwhelming.

Perhaps the first part of this book should conclude where the Pope concludes the first part of *Veritatis Splendor*, reflecting on the Holy Spirit as guarantor of the faith (27). If, but (in important respects) only if, the Pope and the other bishops do eventually confront squarely the fundamental crisis of faith and hope within the Church, they can count on the Spirit's work to make their effort fruitful. The decision to undertake such definitive judgments and such far-reaching reforms of preaching and pastoral practice will itself draw deep on faith. The reaffirmation of the faith in *Veritatis Splendor*, being less definitive and less deep-going, seems unlikely to be as fruitful as John Paul II desires.

ENCYCLICAL LETTER

VERITATIS SPLENDOR

ADDRESSED BY

POPE JOHN PAUL II

TO ALL THE BISHOPS OF THE CATHOLIC
CHURCH REGARDING CERTAIN FUNDAMENTAL
QUESTIONS OF THE CHURCH'S MORAL TEACHING

CONTENTS

CHAPTER TWO

"DO NOT BE CONFORMED
TO THIS WORLD" (*Rom* 12:2)

*The Church and the discernment of certain tendencies in present-day
moral theology*

CHAPTER THREE

"LEST THE CROSS OF CHRIST BE EMPTIED OF ITS POWER" (1 *Cor* 1:17)

Moral good for the life of the Church and of the world

Venerable Brothers in the Episcopate,
Health and the Apostolic Blessing!

The splendour of truth shines forth in all the works of the Creator and, in a special way, in man, created in the image and likeness of God (cf. *Gen* 1:26). Truth enlightens man's intelligence and shapes his freedom, leading him to know and love the Lord. Hence the Psalmist prays: "Let the light of your face shine on us, O Lord" (*Ps* 4:6).

INTRODUCTION

Jesus Christ, the true light that enlightens everyone

1.   Called to salvation through faith in Jesus Christ, "the true light that enlightens everyone" (*Jn* 1:9), people become "light in the Lord" and "children of light" (*Eph* 5:8), and are made holy by "obedience to the truth" (*1 Pet* 1:22).

This obedience is not always easy. As a result of that mysterious original sin, committed at the prompting of Satan, the one who is "a liar and the father of lies" (*Jn* 8:44), man is constantly tempted to turn his gaze away from the living and true God in order to direct it towards idols (cf. *1 Thes* 1:9), exchanging "the truth about God for a lie" (*Rom* 1:25). Man's capacity to know the truth is also darkened, and his will to submit to it is weakened. Thus, giving himself over to relativism and scepticism (cf. *Jn* 18:38), he goes off in search of an illusory freedom apart from truth itself.

But no darkness of error or of sin can totally take away from man the light of God the Creator. In the depths of his heart there always remains a yearning for absolute truth and a thirst to attain full knowledge of it. This is eloquently proved by man's tireless search for knowledge in all fields. It is proved even more by his search for *the meaning of life*. The development of science and technology, this splendid testimony of the human capacity for understanding and for perseverance, does not free humanity from the obligation to ask the ultimate religious questions. Rather, it spurs us on to face the most painful and decisive of struggles, those of the heart and of the moral conscience.

2. No one can escape from the fundamental questions: *What must I do? How do I distinguish good from evil?* The answer is only possible thanks to the splendour of the truth which shines forth deep within the human spirit, as the Psalmist bears witness: "There are many who say: 'O that we might see some good! Let the light of your face shine on us, O Lord'" (*Ps* 4:6).

The light of God's face shines in all its beauty on the contenance of Jesus Christ, "the image of the invisible God" (*Col* 1:15), the "reflection of God's glory" (*Heb* 1:3), "full of grace and truth" (*Jn* 1:14). Christ is "the way, and the truth, and the life" (*Jn* 14:6). Consequently the decisive answer to every one of man's questions, his religious and moral questions in particular, is given by Jesus Christ, or rather is Jesus Christ himself, as the Second Vatican Council recalls: "In fact, *it is only in the mystery of the Word incarnate that light is shed on the mystery of man.* For Adam, the first man, was a figure of the future man, namely, of Christ the Lord. It is Christ, the last Adam, who fully discloses man to himself and unfolds his noble calling by revealing the mystery of the Father and the Father's love".[1]

Jesus Christ, the "light of the nations", shines upon the face of his Church, which he sends forth to the whole world to proclaim the Gospel to every creature (cf. *Mk* 16:15).[2] Hence the Church, as the People of God among the nations,[3] while attentive to the new challenges of history and to mankind's efforts to discover the meaning of life, offers to everyone the answer which comes from the truth about Jesus Christ and his Gospel. The Church remains deeply conscious of her "duty in every age of examining the signs of the times and interpreting them in the light of the Gospel, so that she can offer in a manner appropriate to each generation replies to the continual human questionings on the meaning of this life and the life to come and on how they are related".[4]

3. The Church's Pastors, in communion with the Successor of Peter, are close to the faithful in this effort; they guide and accompany them by their authoritative teaching, finding ever new ways of speaking with love and mercy not only to believers but to all people of good will. The Second Vatican Council remains an extraordinary witness of this

---

[1] Pastoral Constitution on the Church in the Modern World *Gaudium et Spes*, 22.

[2] Cf. SECOND VATICAN ECUMENICAL COUNCIL, Dogmatic Constitution on the Church *Lumen Gentium*, 1.

[3] Cf. *ibid.*, 9.

[4] SECOND VATICAN ECUMENICAL COUNCIL, Pastoral Constitution on the Church in the Modern World *Gaudium et Spes*, 4.

attitude on the part of the Church which, as an "expert in humanity",[5] places herself at the service of every individual and of the whole world.[6]

The Church knows that the issue of morality is one which deeply touches every person; it involves all people, even those who do not know Christ and his Gospel or God himself. She knows that it is precisely *on the path of the moral life that the way of salvation is open to all*. The Second Vatican Council clearly recalled this when it stated that "those who without any fault do not know anything about Christ or his Church, yet who search for God with a sincere heart and under the influence of grace, try to put into effect the will of God as known to them through the dictate of conscience . . . can obtain eternal salvation". The Council added: "Nor does divine Providence deny the helps that are necessary for salvation to those who, through no fault of their own have not yet attained to the express recognition of God, yet who strive, not without divine grace, to lead an upright life. For whatever goodness and truth is found in them is considered by the Church as a preparation for the Gospel and bestowed by him who enlightens everyone that they may in the end have life".[7]

The purpose of the present Encyclical

4.   At all times, but particularly in the last two centuries, the Popes, whether individually or together with the College of Bishops, have developed and proposed a moral teaching regarding the *many different spheres of human life*. In Christ's name and with his authority they have exhorted, passed judgment and explained. In their efforts on behalf of humanity, in fidelity to their mission, they have confirmed, supported and consoled. With the guarantee of assistance from the Spirit of truth they have contributed to a better understanding of moral demands in the areas of human sexuality, the family, and social, economic and political life. In the tradition of the Church and in the history of humanity, their teaching repesents a constant deepening of knowledge with regard to morality.[8]

[5] PAUL VI, *Address* to the General Assembly of the United Nations (4 October 1965), 1: *AAS* 57 (1965), 878; cf. Encyclical Letter *Populorum Progressio* (26 March 1967), 13: *AAS* 59 (1967), 263–264.

[6] Cf. SECOND VATICAN ECUMENICAL COUNCIL, Pastoral Constitution on the Church in the Modern World *Gaudium et Spes*, 16.

[7] Dogmatic Constitution on the Church *Lumen Gentium*, 16.

[8] Pius XII had already pointed out this doctrinal development: cf. *Radio Message* for the Fiftieth Anniversary of the Encyclical Letter *Rerum Novarum* of Leo XIII (1 June 1941): *AAS* 33 (1941), 195–205. Also JOHN XXIII, Encyclical Letter *Mater et Magistra* (15 May 1961): *AAS* 53 (1961), 410–413.

Today, however, it seems *necessary to reflect on the whole of the Church's moral teaching*, with the precise goal of recalling certain fundamental truths of Catholic doctrine which, in the present circumstances, risk being distorted or denied. In fact, a new situation has come about *within the Christian community itself*, which has experienced the spread of numerous doubts and objections of a human and psychological, social and cultural, religious and even properly theological nature, with regard to the Church's moral teachings. It is no longer a matter of limited and occasional dissent, but of an overall and systematic calling into question of traditional moral doctrine, on the basis of certain anthropological and ethical presuppositions. At the root of these presuppositions is the more or less obvious influence of currents of thought which end by detaching human freedom from its essential and constitutive relationship to truth. Thus the traditional doctrine regarding the natural law, and the universality and the permanent validity of its precepts, is rejected; certain of the Church's moral teachings are found simply unacceptable, and the Magisterium itself is considered capable of intervening in matters of morality only in order to "exhort consciences" and to "propose values", in the light of which each individual will independently make his or her decisions and life choices.

In particular, note should be taken of the *lack of harmony between the traditional response of the Church and certain theological positions*, encountered even in Seminaries and in Faculties of Theology, *with regard to questions of the greatest importance* for the Church and for the life of faith of Christians, as well as for the life of society itself. In particular, the question is asked: do the comandments of God, which are written on the human heart and are part of the Covenant, really have the capacity to clarify the daily decisions of individuals and entire societies? Is it possible to obey God and thus love God and neighbour, without respecting these commandments in all circumstances? Also, an opinion is frequently heard which questions the intrinsic and unbreakable bond between faith and morality, as if membership in the Church and her internal unity were to be decided on the basis of faith alone, while in the sphere of morality a pluralism of opinions and of kinds of behaviour could be tolerated, these being left to the judgment of the individual subjective conscience or to the diversity of social and cultural contexts.

5. Given these circumstances, which still exist, I came to the decision—as I announced in my Apostolic Letter *Spiritus Domini*, issued on 1 August 1987 on the second centenary of the death of Saint Alphonsus Maria de' Liguori—to write an Encyclical with the aim of treating "more fully and more deeply the issues regarding the very

foundations of moral theology",[9] foundations which are being under-
mined by certain present-day tendencies.

I address myself to you, Venerable Brothers in the Episcopate, who
share with me the responsibility of safeguarding "sound teaching" (2 *Tim*
4:3), with the intention of *clearly setting forth certain aspects of doctrine which
are of crucial importance in facing what is certainly a genuine crisis*, since the
difficulties which it engenders have most serious implications for the
moral life of the faithful and for communion in the Church, as well as
for a just and fraternal social life.

If this Encyclical, so long awaited, is being published only now, one
of the reasons is that it seemed fitting for it to be preceded by the
Catechism of the Catholic Church, which contains a complete and systematic
exposition of Christian moral teaching. The Catechism presents the
moral life of believers in its fundamental elements and in its many aspects
as the life of the "children of God": "Recognizing in the faith their new
dignity, Christians are called to lead henceforth a life 'worthy of the
Gospel of Christ' (*Phil* 1:27). Through the sacraments and prayer they
receive the grace of Christ and the gifts of his Spirit which make them
capable of such a life".[10] Consequently, while referring back to the
Catechism "as a sure and authentic reference text for teaching Catholic
doctrine",[11] the Encyclical will limit itself to dealing with *certain fundamental questions regarding the Church's moral teaching*, taking the form of a
necessary discernment about issues being debated by ethicists and moral
theologians. The specific purpose of the present Encyclical is this: to set
forth, with regard to the problems being discussed, the principles of a
moral teaching based upon Sacred Scripture and the living Apostolic
Tradition,[12] and at the same time to shed light on the presuppositions
and consequences of the dissent which that teaching has met.

---

[4] Apostolic Letter *Spiritus Domini* (1 August 1987): *AAS* 79 (1987), 1374.

[10] *Catechism of the Catholic Church*, No. 1692.

[11] Apostolic Constitution *Fidei Depositum* (11 October 1992), 4.

[12] Cf. SECOND VATICAN ECUMENICAL COUNCIL, Dogmatic Constitution on Divine
Revelation *Dei Verbum*, 10.

CHAPTER ONE

"TEACHER, WHAT GOOD MUST I DO ...?"

(*Mt* 19:16)

CHRIST AND THE ANSWER TO THE QUESTION ABOUT MORALITY

"Someone came to him ..." (*Mt* 19:16)

6. *The dialogue of Jesus with the rich young man,* related in the nineteenth chapter of Saint Matthew's Gospel, can serve as a useful guide *for listening once more* in a lively and direct way to his moral teaching: "Then someone came to him and said, 'Teacher, what good must I do to have eternal life?' And he said to him, 'Why do you ask me about what is good? There is only one who is good. If you wish to enter into life, keep the commandments.' He said to him, 'Which ones?' And Jesus said, 'You shall not murder; You shall not commit adultery; You shall not steal; You shall not bear false witness; Honour your father and mother; also, You shall love your neighbour as yourself.' The young man said to him, 'I have kept all these; what do I still lack?' Jesus said to him, 'If you wish to be perfect, go, sell your possessions and give the money to the poor, and you will have treasure in heaven; then come, follow me'" (*Mt* 19:16–21).[13]

---

[13] Cf. Apostolic Epistle *Parati semper* to the Young People of the World on the occasion of the International Year of Youth (31 March 1985), 2–8: *AAS* 77 (1985), 581–600.

7. *"Then someone came to him . . ."*. In the young man, whom Matthew's Gospel does not name, we can recognize every person who, consciously or not, *approaches Christ the Redeemer of man and questions him about morality*. For the young man, the *question* is not so much about rules to be followed, but *about the full meaning of life*. This is in fact the aspiration at the heart of every human decision and action, the quiet searching and interior prompting which sets freedom in motion. This question is ultimately an appeal to the absolute Good which attracts us and beckons us; it is the echo of a call from God who is the origin and goal of man's life. Precisely in this perspective the Second Vatican Council called for a renewal of moral theology, so that its teaching would display the lofty vocation which the faithful have received in Christ,[14] the only response fully capable of satisfying the desire of the human heart.

In order to make this "encounter" with Christ possible, God willed his Church. Indeed, the Church "wishes to serve this single end: that each person may be able to find Christ, in order that Christ may walk with each person the path of life".[15]

"Teacher, what good must I do to have eternal life?" (*Mt* 19:16)

8. The question which the rich young man puts to Jesus of Nazareth is one which rises from the depths of his heart. It is *an essential and unavoidable question for the life of every man*, for it is about the moral good which must be done, and about eternal life. The young man senses that there is a connection between moral good and the fulfilment of his own destiny. He is a devout Israelite, raised as it were in the shadow of the Law of the Lord. If he asks Jesus this question, we can presume that it is not because he is ignorant of the answer contained in the Law. It is more likely that the attractiveness of the person of Jesus had prompted within him new questions about moral good. He feels the need to draw near to the One who had begun his preaching with this new and decisive proclamation: "The time is fulfilled, and the Kingdom of God is at hand; repent, and believe in the Gospel" (*Mk* 1:15).

People today need to turn to Christ once again in order to receive from him the answer to their questions about what is good and what is evil. Christ is the Teacher, the Risen One who has life in himself and who is always

---

[14] Cf. Decree on Priestly Formation *Optatam Totius*, 16.
[15] Encyclical Letter *Redemptor Hominis* (4 March 1979), 13: *AAS* 71 (1979), 282.

present in his Church and in the world. It is he who opens up to the faithful the book of the Scriptures and, by fully revealing the Father's will, teaches the truth about moral action. At the source and summit of the economy of salvation, as the Alpha and the Omega of human history (cf. *Rev* 1:8, 21:6; 22:13), Christ sheds light on man's condition and his integral vocation. Consequently, "the man who wishes to understand himself thoroughly—and not just in accordance with immediate, partial, often superficial, and even illusory standards and measures of his being—must with his unrest, uncertainty and even his weakness and sinfulness, with his life and death, draw near to Christ. He must, so to speak, enter him with all his own self; he must 'appropriate' and assimilate the whole of the reality of the Incarnation and Redemption in order to find himself. If this profound process takes place within him, he then bears fruit not only of adoration of God but also of deeper wonder at himself".[16]

If we therefore wish to go to the heart of the Gospel's moral teaching and grasp its profound and unchanging content, we must carefully inquire into the meaning of the question asked by the rich young man in the Gospel and, even more, the meaning of Jesus' reply, allowing ourselves to be guided by him. Jesus, as a patient and sensitive teacher, answers the young man by taking him, as it were, by the hand, and leading him step by step to the full truth.

"There is only one who is good" (*Mt* 19:17)

9.   Jesus says: "Why do you ask me about what is good? There is only one who is good. If you wish to enter into life, keep the commandments" (*Mt* 19:17). In the versions of the Evangelists Mark and Luke the question is phrased in this way: "Why do you call me good? No one is good but God alone" (*Mk* 10:18; cf. *Lk* 18:19).

Before answering the question, Jesus wishes the young man to have a clear idea of why he asked his question. The "Good Teacher" points out to him—and to all of us—that the answer to the question, "What good must I do to have eternal life?" can only be found by turning one's mind and heart to the "One" who is good: "No one is good but God alone" (*Mk* 10:18; cf. *Lk* 18:19). *Only God can answer the question about what is good, because he is the Good itself.*

To ask about the good, in fact, *ultimately means to turn towards God*, the fullness of goodness. Jesus shows that the young man's question is really a *religious question*, and that the goodness that attracts and at the same time obliges man has its source in God, and indeed is God himself. God alone

[16]   *Ibid.*, 10: *loc. cit.*, 274.

is worthy of being loved "with all one's heart, and with all one's soul, and with all one's mind" (*Mt* 22:37). He is the source of man's happiness. Jesus brings the question about morally good action back to its religious foundations, to the acknowledgment of God, who alone is goodness, fullness of life, the final end of human activity, and perfect happiness.

10. The Church, instructed by the Teacher's words, believes that man, made in the image of the Creator, redeemed by the Blood of Christ and made holy by the presence of the Holy Spirit, has as the *ultimate purpose* of his life *to live "for the praise of God's glory"* (cf. *Eph* 1:12), striving to make each of his actions reflect the splendour of that glory. "Know, then, O beautiful soul, that you are *the image of God* ", writes Saint Ambrose. "Know that you are *the glory of God* (1 *Cor* 11:7). Hear how you are his glory. The Prophet says: *Your knowledge has become too wonderful for me* (cf. *Ps.* 138:6, Vulg.). That is to say, in my work your majesty has become more wonderful; in the counsels of men your wisdom is exalted. When I consider myself, such as I am known to you in my secret thoughts and deepest emotions, the mysteries of your knowledge are disclosed to me. Know then, O man, your greatness, and be vigilant".[17]

What man is and what he must do becomes clear as soon as God reveals himself. The Decalogue is based on these words: "I am the Lord your God, who brought you out of the land of Egypt, out of the house of bondage" (*Ex* 20:2–3). In the "ten words" of the Covenant with Israel, and in the whole Law, God makes himself known and acknowledged as the One who "alone is good"; the One who despite man's sin remains the "model" for moral action, in accordance with his command, "You shall be holy; for I the Lord your God am holy" (*Lev* 19:2); as the One who, faithful to his love for man, gives him his Law (cf. *Ex* 19:9–24 and 20:18–21) in order to restore man's original and peaceful harmony with the Creator and with all creation, and, what is more, to draw him into his divine love: "I will walk among you, and will be your God, and you shall be my people" (*Lev* 26:12).

The moral life presents itself as the response due to the many gratuitous initiatives taken by God out of love for man. It is a response of love, according to the statement made in Deuteronomy about the fundamental commandment: "Hear, O Israel: The Lord our God is one Lord; and you shall love the Lord your God with all your heart, and with all your soul, and with all your might. And these words which I command you this day shall be upon your heart; and you shall teach them diligently to your children" (*Dt* 6:4–7). Thus the moral life, caught up in the gratuitousness of God's love, is called to reflect his glory: "For the one who loves God

---

[17] *Exameron*, Dies VI, Sermo IX, 8, 50: *CSEL* 32, 241.

it is enough to be pleasing to the One whom he loves: for no greater reward should be sought than that love itself; charity in fact is of God in such a way that God himself is charity".[18]

11.   The statement that "There is only one who is good" thus brings us back to the "first tablet" of the commandments, which calls us to acknowledge God as the one Lord of all and to worship him alone for his infinite holiness (cf. *Ex* 20:2–11). *The good is belonging to God, obeying him*, walking humbly with him in doing justice and in loving kindness (cf. *Mic* 6:8). *Acknowledging the Lord as God is the very core, the heart of the Law*, from which the particular precepts flow and towards which they are ordered. In the morality of the commandments the fact that the people of Israel belongs to the Lord is made evident, because God alone is the One who is good. Such is the witness of Sacred Scripture, imbued in every one of its pages with a lively perception of God's absolute holiness: "Holy, holy, holy is the Lord of hosts" (*Is* 6:3).

But if God alone is the Good, no human effort, not even the most rigorous observance of the commandments, succeeds in "fulfilling" the Law, that is, acknowledging the Lord as God and rendering him the worship due to him alone (cf. *Mt* 4:10). *This "fulfilment" can come only from a gift of God:* the offer of a share in the divine Goodness revealed and communicated in Jesus, the one whom the rich young man addresses with the words "Good Teacher" (*Mk* 10:17; *Lk* 18:18). What the young man now perhaps only dimly perceives will in the end be fully revealed by Jesus himself in the invitation: "Come, follow me" (*Mt* 19:21).

"If you wish to enter into life, keep the commandments" (*Mt* 19:17)

12.   Only God can answer the question about the good, because he is the Good. But God has already given an answer to this question: he did so *by creating man and ordering him* with wisdom and love to his final end, through the law which is inscribed in his heart (cf. *Rom* 2:15), the "natural law". The latter "is nothing other than the light of understanding infused in us by God, whereby we understand what must be done and what must be avoided. God gave this light and this law to man at creation".[19] He also did so *in the history of Israel*, particularly in the "ten

---

[18] SAINT LEO THE GREAT, *Sermo XCII*, Chap. III: *PL* 54, 454.

[19] SAINT THOMAS AQUINAS, *In Duo Praecepta Caritatis et in Decem Legis Praecepta. Prologus: Opuscula Theologica*, II, No. 1129, Ed. Taurinen. (1954), 245; cf. *Summa Theologiae*, I–II, q. 91, a. 2; *Catechism of the Catholic Church*, No. 1955.

words", the *commandments of Sinai*, whereby he brought into existence the people of the Covenant (cf. *Ex* 24) and called them to be his "own possession among all peoples", "a holy nation" (*Ex* 19:5–6), which would radiate his holiness to all peoples (cf. *Wis* 18:4; *Ez* 20:41). The gift of the Decalogue was a promise and sign of the *New Covenant*, in which the law would be written in a new and definitive way upon the human heart (cf. *Jer* 31:31–34), replacing the law of sin which had disfigured that heart (cf. *Jer* 17:1). In those days, "a new heart" would be given, for in it would dwell "a new spirit", the Spirit of God (cf. *Ez* 36:24–28).[20]

Consequently, after making the important clarification: "There is only one who is good", Jesus tells the young man: "If you wish to enter into life, keep the commandments" (*Mt* 19:17). In this way, a close connection is made *between eternal life and obedience to God's commandments*: God's commandments show man the path of life and they lead to it. From the very lips of Jesus, the new Moses, man is once again given the commandments of the Decalogue. Jesus himself definitively confirms them and proposes them to us as the way and condition of salvation. *The commandments are linked to a promise.* In the Old Covenant the object of the promise was the possession of a land where the people would be able to live in freedom and in accordance with righteousness (cf. *Dt* 6:20–25). In the New Covenant the object of the promise is the "Kingdom of Heaven", as Jesus declares at the beginning of the "Sermon on the Mount"—a sermon which contains the fullest and most complete formulation of the New Law (cf. *Mt* 5—7), clearly linked to the Decalogue entrusted by God to Moses on Mount Sinai. This same reality of the Kingdom is referred to in the expression "eternal life", which is a participation in the very life of God. It is attained in its perfection only after death, but in faith it is even now a light of truth, a source of meaning for life, an inchoate share in the full following of Christ. Indeed, Jesus says to his disciples after speaking to the rich young man: "Every one who has left houses or brothers or sisters or father or mother or children or lands, for my name's sake, will receive a hundredfold and inherit eternal life" (*Mt* 19:29).

13. Jesus' answer is not enough for the young man, who continues by asking the Teacher about the commandments which must be kept: "He said to him, 'Which ones?'" (*Mt* 19:18). He asks what he must do in life in order to show that he acknowledges God's holiness. After directing the young man's gaze towards God, Jesus reminds him of the commandments of the Decalogue regarding one's neighbour: "Jesus said: 'You

[20] Cf. SAINT MAXIMUS THE CONFESSOR, *Quaestiones ad Thalassium*, Q. 64: PG 90, 723–728.

shall not murder; You shall not commit adultery; You shall not bear false witness; Honour your father and mother; also, You shall love your neighbour as yourself'" (*Mt* 19:18–19).

From the context of the conversation, and especially from a comparison of Matthew's text with the parallel passages in Mark and Luke, it is clear that Jesus does not intend to list each and every one of the commandments required in order to "enter into life", but rather wishes to draw the young man's attention to the *"centrality" of the Decalogue* with regard to every other precept, inasmuch as it is the interpretation of what the words "I am the Lord your God" mean for man. Nevertheless we cannot fail to notice which commandments of the Law the Lord recalls to the young man. They are some of the commandments belonging to the so-called "second tablet" of the Decalogue, the summary (cf. *Rom* 13:8–10) and foundation of which is *the commandment of love of neighbour:* "You shall love your neighbour as yourself" (*Mt* 19:19; cf. *Mk* 12:31). In this commandment we find a precise expression of *the singular dignity of the human person,* "the only creature that God has wanted for its own sake".[21] The different commandments of the Decalogue are really only so many reflections of the one commandment about the good of the person, at the level of the many different goods which characterize his identity as a spiritual and bodily being in relationship with God, with his neighbour and with the material world. As we read in the *Catechism of the Catholic Church,* "the Ten Commandments are part of God's Revelation. At the same time, they teach us man's true humanity. They shed light on the essential duties, and so indirectly on the fundamental rights, inherent in the nature of the human person".[22]

The commandments of which Jesus reminds the young man are meant to safeguard *the good* of the person, the image of God, by protecting his *goods.* "You shall not murder; You shall not commit adultery; You shall not steal; You shall not bear false witness" are moral rules formulated in terms of prohibitions. These negative precepts express with particular force the ever urgent need to protect human life, the communion of persons in marriage, private property, truthfulness and people's good name.

The commandments thus represent the basic condition for love of neighbour; at the same time they are the proof of that love. They are the *first necessary step on the journey towards freedom,* its starting-point. "The beginning of freedom", Saint Augustine writes, "is to be free from crimes . . . such as murder, adultery, fornication, theft, fraud, sacrilege

---

[21] SECOND VATICAN ECUMENICAL COUNCIL, Pastoral Constitution on the Church in the Modern World *Gaudium et Spes,* 24.

[22] *Catechism of the Catholic Church,* No. 2070.

and so forth. When once one is without these crimes (and every Christian should be without them), one begins to lift up one's head towards freedom. But this is only the beginning of freedom, not perfect freedom . . .".[23]

14. This certainly does not mean that Christ wishes to put the love of neighbour higher than, or even to set it apart from, the love of God. This is evident from his conversation with the teacher of the Law, who asked him a question very much like the one asked by the young man. Jesus refers him to *the two commandments of love of God and love of neighbour* (cf. *Lk* 10:25–27), and reminds him that only by observing them will he have eternal life: "Do this, and you will live" (*Lk* 10:28). Nonetheless it is significant that it is precisely the second of these commandments which arouses the curiosity of the teacher of the Law, who asks him: "And who is my neighbour?" (*Lk* 10:29). The Teacher replies with the parable of the Good Samaritan, which is critical for fully understanding the commandment of love of neighbour (cf. *Lk* 10:30–37).

These two commandments, on which "depend all the Law and the Prophets" (*Mt* 22:40), are profoundly connected and mutually related. *Their inseparable unity* is attested to by Christ in his words and by his very life: his mission culminates in the Cross of our Redemption (cf. *Jn* 3:14–15), the sign of his indivisible love for the Father and for humanity (cf. *Jn* 13:1).

Both the Old and the New Testaments explicitly affirm that *without love of neighbour*, made concrete in keeping the commandments, *genuine love for God is not possible*. Saint John makes the point with extraordinary forcefulness: "If anyone says, 'I love God', and hates his brother, he is a liar; for he who does not love his brother whom he has seen, cannot love God whom he has not seen" (*1 Jn* 4:20). The Evangelist echoes the moral preaching of Christ, expressed in a wonderful and unambiguous way in the parable of the Good Samaritan (cf. *Lk* 10:30–37) and in his words about the final judgment (cf. *Mt* 25:31–46).

15. In the "Sermon on the Mount", the *magna charta* of Gospel morality,[24] Jesus says: "Do not think that I have come to abolish the Law and the Prophets; I have come not to abolish them but to fulfil them" (*Mt* 5:17). Christ is the key to the Scriptures: "You search the Scriptures . . .; and it is they that bear witness to me" (*Jn* 5:39). Christ is the centre of the economy of salvation, the recapitulation of the Old and New Testaments, of the promises of the Law and of their fulfilment in

---

[23] *In Iohannis Evangelium Tractatus*, 41, 10: *CCL* 36, 363.
[24] Cf. SAINT AUGUSTINE, *De Sermone Domini in Monte*, I, 1, 1: *CCL* 35, 1–2.

the Gospel; he is the living and eternal link between the Old and New Covenants. Commenting on Paul's statement that "Christ is the end of the law" (*Rom* 10:4), Saint Ambrose writes: "end not in the sense of a deficiency, but in the sense of the fullness of the Law: a fullness which is achieved in Christ (*plenitudo legis in Christo est*), since he came not to abolish the Law but to bring it to fulfilment. In the same way that there is an Old Testament, but all truth is in the New Testament, so it is for the Law: what was given through Moses is a figure of the true law. Therefore, the Mosaic Law is an image of the truth".[25]

Jesus brings God's commandments to fulfilment, particularly the commandment of love of neighbour, *by interiorizing their demands and by bringing out their fullest meaning*. Love of neighbour springs from *a loving heart* which, precisely because it loves, is ready to live out *the loftiest challenges*. Jesus shows that the commandments must not be understood as a minimum limit not to be gone beyond, but rather as a path involving a moral and spiritual journey towards perfection, at the heart of which is love (cf. *Col* 3:14). Thus the commandment "You shall not murder" becomes a call to an attentive love which protects and promotes the life of one's neighbour. The precept prohibiting adultery becomes an invitation to a pure way of looking at others, capable of respecting the spousal meaning of the body: "You have heard that it was said to the men of old, '*You shall not kill*; and whoever kills shall be liable to judgment'. *But I say to you* that every one who is angry with his brother shall be liable to judgment . . . You have heard that it was said, '*You shall not commit adultery*'. *But I say to you* that every one who looks at a woman lustfully has already committed adultery with her in his heart" (*Mt* 5:21–22, 27–28). *Jesus himself is the living "fulfilment" of the Law* inasmuch as he fulfils its authentic meaning by the total gift of himself: *he himself becomes a living and personal Law*, who invites people to follow him; through the Spirit, he gives the grace to share his own life and love and provides the strength to bear witness to that love in personal choices and actions (cf. *Jn* 13:34–35).

"If you wish to be perfect" (*Mt* 19:21)

16. The answer he receives about the commandments does not satisfy the young man, who asks Jesus a further question. "I have kept all these; *what do I still lack?*" (*Mt* 19:20). It is not easy to say with a clear conscience "I have kept all these", if one has any understanding of the

---

[25] *In Psalmum CXVIII Expositio*, Sermo 18, 37: *PL* 15, 1541; cf. SAINT CHROMATIUS OF AQUILEIA, *Tractatus in Matthaeum*, XX, I, 1–4: *CCL* 9/A, 291–292.

real meaning of the demands contained in God's Law. And yet, even though he is able to make this reply, even though he has followed the moral ideal seriously and generously from childhood, the rich young man knows that he is still far from the goal: before the person of Jesus he realizes that he is still lacking something. It is his awareness of this insufficiency that Jesus addresses in his final answer. Conscious of *the young man's yearning for something greater, which would transcend a legalistic interpretation of the commandments,* the Good Teacher invites him to enter upon the path of perfection: "If you wish to be perfect, go, sell your possessions and give the money to the poor, and you will have treasure in heaven; then come, follow me" (*Mt* 19:21).

Like the earlier part of Jesus' answer, this part too must be read and interpreted in the context of the whole moral message of the Gospel, and in particular in the context of the Sermon on the Mount, the Beatitudes (cf. *Mt* 5:3–12), the first of which is precisely the Beatitude of the poor, the "poor in spirit" as Saint Matthew makes clear (*Mt* 5:3), the humble. In this sense it can be said that the Beatitudes are also relevant to the answer given by Jesus to the young man's question: "What good must I do to have eternal life?" Indeed, each of the Beatitudes promises, from a particular viewpoint, that very "good" which opens man up to eternal life, and indeed is eternal life.

The Beatitudes are not specifically concerned with certain particular rules of behaviour. Rather, they speak of basic attitudes and dispositions in life and therefore they *do not coincide exactly with the commandments.* On the other hand, *there is no separation or opposition* between the Beatitudes and the commandments: both refer to the good, to eternal life. The Sermon on the Mount begins with the proclamation of the Beatitudes, but also refers to the commandments (cf. *Mt* 5:20–48). At the same time, the Sermon on the Mount demonstrates the openness of the commandments and their orientation towards the horizon of the perfection proper to the Beatitudes. These latter are above all *promises,* from which there also indirectly flow *normative indications* for the moral life. In their originality and profundity they are a sort of *self-portrait of Christ,* and for this very reason are *invitations to discipleship and to communion of life with Christ.*[26]

17.   We do not know how clearly the young man in the Gospel understood the profound and challenging import of Jesus' first reply: "If you wish to enter into life, keep the commandments". But it is certain that the young man's commitment to respect all the moral demands of the commandments represents the absolutely essential ground in which the desire for perfection can take root and mature, the desire, that is, for

---

[26] Cf. *Catechism of the Catholic Church,* No. 1717.

the meaning of the commandments to be completely fulfilled in following Christ. Jesus' conversation with the young man helps us to grasp *the conditions for the moral growth of man, who has been called to perfection*: the young man, having observed all the commandments, shows that he is incapable of taking the next step by himself alone. To do so requires mature human freedom ("If you wish to be perfect") and God's gift of grace ("Come, follow me").

Perfection demands that maturity in self-giving to which human freedom is called. Jesus points out to the young man that the commandments are the first and indispensable condition for having eternal life; on the other hand, for the young man to give up all he possesses and to follow the Lord is presented as an invitation: "If you wish . . .". These words of Jesus reveal the particular dynamic of freedom's growth towards maturity, and at the same time *they bear witness to the fundamental relationship between freedom and divine law*. Human freedom and God's law are not in opposition; on the contrary, they appeal one to the other. The follower of Christ knows that his vocation is to freedom. "You were called to freedom, brethren" (*Gal* 5:13), proclaims the Apostle Paul with joy and pride. But he immediately adds: "only do not use your freedom as an opportunity for the flesh, but through love be servants of one another" (*ibid.*). The firmness with which the Apostle opposes those who believe that they are justified by the Law has nothing to do with man's "liberation" from precepts. On the contrary, the latter are at the service of the practice of love: "For he who loves his neighbour has fulfilled the Law. The commandments, '*You shall not commit adultery; You shall not murder; You shall not steal; You shall not covet,*' and any other commandment, are summed up in this sentence, '*You shall love your neighbour as yourself*'" (*Rom* 13:8–9). Saint Augustine, after speaking of the observance of the commandments as being a kind of incipient, imperfect freedom, goes on to say: "Why, someone will ask, is it not yet perfect? Because 'I see in my members another law at war with the law of my reason' . . . In part freedom, in part slavery: not yet complete freedom, not yet pure, not yet whole, because we are not yet in eternity. In part we retain our weakness and in part we have attained freedom. All our sins were destroyed in Baptism, but does it follow that no weakness remained after iniquity was destroyed? Had none remained, we would live without sin in this life. But who would dare to say this except someone who is proud, someone unworthy of the mercy of our deliverer? . . . Therefore, since some weakness has remained in us, I dare to say that to the extent to which we serve God we are free, while to the extent that we follow the law of sin, we are still slaves".[27]

---

[27] *In Iohannis Evangelium Tractatus*, 41, 10: CCL 36, 363.

18. Those who live "by the flesh" experience God's law as a burden, and indeed as a denial or at least a restriction of their own freedom. On the other hand, those who are impelled by love and "walk by the Spirit" (*Gal* 5:16), and who desire to serve others, find in God's Law the fundamental and necessary way in which to practise love as something freely chosen and freely lived out. Indeed, they feel an interior urge—a genuine "necessity" and no longer a form of coercion—not to stop at the minimum demands of the Law, but to live them in their "fullness". This is a still uncertain and fragile journey as long as we are on earth, but it is one made possible by grace, which enables us to possess the full freedom of the children of God (cf. *Rom* 8:21) and thus to live our moral life in a way worthy of our sublime vocation as "sons in the Son".

This vocation to perfect love is not restricted to a small group of individuals. *The invitation*, "go, sell your possessions and give the money to the poor", and the promise "you will have treasure in heaven", *are meant for everyone*, because they bring out the full meaning of the commandment of love for neighbour, just as the invitation which follows, "Come, follow me", is the new, specific form of the command-ment of love of God. Both the commandments and Jesus' invitation to the rich young man stand at the service of a single and indivisible charity, which spontaneously tends towards that perfection whose measure is God alone: "You, therefore, must be perfect, as your heavenly Father is perfect" (*Mt* 5:48). In the Gospel of Luke, Jesus makes even clearer the meaning of this perfection: "Be merciful, even as your Father is merciful" (*Lk* 6:36).

"Come, follow me" (*Mt* 19:21)

19. The way and at the same time the content of this perfection consist in the following of Jesus, *sequela Christi*, once one has given up one's own wealth and very self. This is precisely the conclusion of Jesus' conversation with the young man: "Come, follow me" (*Mt* 19:21). It is an invitation the marvellous grandeur of which will be fully perceived by the disciples after Christ's Resurrection, when the Holy Spirit leads them to all truth (cf. *Jn* 16:13).

It is Jesus himself who takes the initiative and calls people to follow him. His call is addressed first to those to whom he entrusts a particular mission, beginning with the Twelve; but it is also clear that every believer is called to be a follower of Christ (cf. *Acts* 6:1). *Following Christ is thus the essential and primordial foundation of Christian morality*: just as the people of Israel followed God who led them through the desert towards the Promised Land (cf. *Ex* 13:21), so every disciple must follow Jesus, towards whom he is drawn by the Father himself (cf. *Jn* 6:44).

This is not a matter only of disposing oneself to hear a teaching and obediently accepting a commandment. More radically, it involves *holding fast to the very person of Jesus*, partaking of his life and his destiny, sharing in his free and loving obedience to the will of the Father. By responding in faith and following the one who is Incarnate Wisdom, the disciple of Jesus truly becomes *a disciple of God* (cf. *Jn* 6:45). Jesus is indeed the light of the world, the light of life (cf. *Jn* 8:12). He is the shepherd who leads his sheep and feeds them (cf. *Jn* 10:11–16); he is the way, and the truth, and the life (cf. *Jn* 14:6). It is Jesus who leads to the Father, so much so that to see him, the Son, is to see the Father (cf. *Jn* 14:6–10). And thus to imitate the Son, "the image of the invisible God" (*Col* 1:15), means to imitate the Father.

20. *Jesus asks us to follow him and to imitate him along the path of love, a love which gives itself completely to the brethren out of love for God:* "This is my commandment, that you love one another as I have loved you" (*Jn* 15:12). The word "as" requires imitation of Jesus and of his love, of which the washing of feet is a sign: "If I then, your Lord and Teacher, have washed your feet, you also ought to wash one another's feet. For I have given you an example, that you should do as I have done to you" (*Jn* 13:14–15). Jesus' way of acting and his words, his deeds and his precepts constitute the moral rule of Christian life. Indeed, his actions, and in particular his Passion and Death on the Cross, are the living revelation of his love for the Father and for others. This is exactly the love that Jesus wishes to be imitated by all who follow him. It is *the "new" commandment*: "A new commandment I give to you, that you love one another; even as I have loved you, that you also love one another. By this all men will know that you are my disciples, if you have love for one another" (*Jn* 13:34–35).

The word "as" also indicates the *degree* of Jesus' love, and of the love with which his disciples are called to love one another. After saying: "This is my commandment, that you love one another as I have loved you" (*Jn* 15:12), Jesus continues with words which indicate the sacrificial gift of his life on the Cross, as the witness to a love "to the end" (*Jn* 13:1): "Greater love has no man than this, that a man lay down his life for his friends" (*Jn* 15:13).

As he calls the young man to follow him along the way of perfection, Jesus asks him to be perfect in the command of love, in "his" command-ment: to become part of the unfolding of his complete giving, to imitate and rekindle the very love of the "Good" Teacher, the one who loved "to the end". This is what Jesus asks of everyone who wishes to follow him: "If any man would come after me, let him deny himself and take up his cross and follow me" (*Mt* 16:24).

21.   *Following Christ* is not an outward imitation, since it touches man at the very depths of his being. Being a follower of Christ means *becoming conformed to him* who became a servant even to giving himself on the Cross (cf. *Phil* 2:5–8). Christ dwells by faith in the heart of the believer (cf. *Eph* 3:17), and thus the disciple is conformed to the Lord. This is the *effect of grace*, of the active presence of the Holy Spirit in us.

Having become one with Christ, the Christian *becomes a member of his Body, which is the Church* (cf. *1 Cor* 12:13, 27). By the work of the Spirit, Baptism radically configures the faithful to Christ in the Paschal Mystery of death and resurrection; it "clothes him" in Christ (cf. *Gal* 3:27): "Let us rejoice and give thanks", exclaims Saint Augustine speaking to the baptized, "for we have become not only Christians, but Christ (. . .). Marvel and rejoice: we have become Christ!"[28] Having died to sin, those who are baptized receive new life (cf. *Rom* 6:3–11): alive for God in Christ Jesus, they are called to walk by the Spirit and to manifest the Spirit's fruits in their lives (cf. *Gal* 5:16–25). Sharing in the *Eucharist*, the sacrament of the New Covenant (cf. *1 Cor* 11:23–29), is the culmination of our assimilation to Christ, the source of "eternal life" (cf. *Jn* 6:51–58), the source and power of that complete gift of self, which Jesus—according to the testimony handed on by Paul—commands us to commemorate in liturgy and in life: "As often as you eat this bread and drink the cup, you proclaim the Lord's death until he comes" (*1 Cor* 11:26).

"With God all things are possible" (*Mt* 19:26)

22.   The conclusion of Jesus' conversation with the rich young man is very poignant: "When the young man heard this, he went away sorrowful, for he had many possessions" (*Mt* 19:22). Not only the rich man but the disciples themselves are taken aback by Jesus' call to discipleship, the demands of which transcend human aspirations and abilities: "When the disciples heard this, they were greatly astounded and said, 'Then who can be saved?'" (*Mt* 19:25). *But the Master refers them to God's power:* "With men this is impossible, but with God all things are possible" (*Mt* 19:26).

In the same chapter of Matthew's Gospel (19:3–10), Jesus, interpreting the Mosaic Law on marriage, rejects the right to divorce, appealing to a "beginning" more fundamental and more authoritative than the Law of

---

[28]   *Ibid.*, 21, 8: CCL 36, 216.

Moses: God's original plan for mankind, a plan which man after sin has no longer been able to live up to: "For your hardness of heart Moses allowed you to divorce your wives, but from the beginning it was not so" (*Mt* 19:8). Jesus' appeal to the "beginning" dismays the disciples, who remark: "If such is the case of a man with his wife, it is not expedient to marry" (*Mt* 19:10). And Jesus, referring specifically to the charism of celibacy "for the Kingdom of Heaven" (*Mt* 19:12), but stating a general rule, indicates the new and surprising possibility opened up to man by God's grace. "He said to them: 'Not everyone can accept this saying, but only those to whom it is given'" (*Mt* 19:11).

To imitate and live out the love of Christ is not possible for man by his own strength alone. He becomes *capable of this love only by virtue of a gift received*. As the Lord Jesus receives the love of his Father, so he in turn freely communicates that love to his disciples: "As the Father has loved me, so have I loved you; abide in my love" (*Jn* 15:9). *Christ's gift is his Spirit*, whose first "fruit" (cf. *Gal* 5:22) is charity: "God's love has been poured into our hearts through the Holy Spirit which has been given to us" (*Rom* 5:5). Saint Augustine asks: "Does love bring about the keeping of the commandments, or does the keeping of the commandments bring about love?" And he answers: "But who can doubt that love comes first? For the one who does not love has no reason for keeping the commandments".[29]

23. "The law of the Spirit of life in Christ Jesus has set me free from the law of sin and death" (*Rom* 8:2). With these words the Apostle Paul invites us to consider in the perspective of the history of salvation, which reaches its fulfilment in Christ, *the relationship between the* (Old) *Law and grace* (the New Law). He recognizes the pedagogic function of the Law, which, by enabling sinful man to take stock of his own powerlessness and by stripping him of the presumption of his self-sufficiency, leads him to ask for and to receive "life in the Spirit". Only in this new life is it possible to carry out God's commandments. Indeed, it is through faith in Christ that we have been made righteous (cf. *Rom* 3:28): the "righteousness" which the Law demands, but is unable to give, is found by every believer to be revealed and granted by the Lord Jesus. Once again it is Saint Augustine who admirably sums up this Pauline dialectic of law and grace: "The law was given that grace might be sought; and grace was given, that the law might be fulfilled".[30]

Love and life according to the Gospel cannot be thought of first and foremost as a kind of precept, because what they demand is beyond

---

[29] *Ibid.*, 82, 3: CCL 36, 533.
[30] *De Spiritu et Littera*, 19, 34: CSEL 60, 187.

man's abilities. They are possible only as the result of a gift of God who heals, restores and transforms the human heart by his grace: "For the law was given through Moses; grace and truth came through Jesus Christ" (*Jn* 1:17). The promise of eternal life is thus linked to the gift of grace, and the gift of the Spirit which we have received is even now the "guarantee of our inheritance" (*Eph* 1:14).

24. And so we find revealed the authentic and original aspect of the commandment of love and of the perfection to which it is ordered: we are speaking of a *possibility opened up to man exclusively by grace*, by the gift of God, by his love. On the other hand, precisely the awareness of having received the gift, of possessing in Jesus Christ the love of God, generates and sustains *the free response* of a full love for God and the brethren, as the Apostle John insistently reminds us in his first Letter: "Beloved, let us love one another; for love is of God and knows God. He who does not love does not know God; for God is love ... Beloved, if God so loved us, we ought also to love one another ... We love, because he first loved us" (*1 Jn* 4:7–8, 11, 19).

This inseparable connection between the Lord's grace and human freedom, between gift and task, has been expressed in simple yet profound words by Saint Augustine in his prayer: "*Da quod iubes et iube quod vis*" (grant what you command and command what you will).[31]

The gift does not lessen but reinforces the moral demands of love: "This is his commandment, that we should believe in the name of his Son Jesus Christ and love one another just as he has commanded us" (*1 Jn* 3:32). One can "abide" in love only by keeping the commandments, as Jesus states: "If you keep my commandments, you will abide in my love, just as I have kept my Father's commandments and abide in his love" (*Jn* 15:10).

Going to the heart of the moral message of Jesus and the preaching of the Apostles, and summing up in a remarkable way the great tradition of the Fathers of the East and West, and of Saint Augustine in particular,[32] Saint Thomas was able to write that *the New Law is the grace of the Holy Spirit given through faith in Christ*.[33] The external precepts also mentioned in the Gospel dispose one for this grace or produce its effects in one's life. Indeed, the New Law is not content to say what must be done, but also gives the power to "do what is true" (cf. *Jn* 3:21). Saint John Chrysostom likewise observed that the New Law was promulgated at the descent of

---

[31] *Confessiones*, X, 29, 40: CCL 27, 176; cf. *De Gratia et Libero Arbitrio*, XV: PL 44, 899.

[32] Cf. *De Spiritu et Littera*, 21, 36; 26, 46; CSEL 60, 189–190; 200–201.

[33] Cf. *Summa Theologiae*, I–II, q. 106, a. 1 conclusion and ad 2um.

the Holy Spirit from heaven on the day of Pentecost, and that the Apostles "did not come down from the mountain carrying, like Moses, tablets of stone in their hands; but they came down carrying the Holy Spirit in their hearts . . . having become by his grace a living law, a living book".[34]

"Lo, I am with you always, to the close of the age"
(Mt 28:20)

25. Jesus' conversation with the rich young man continues, in a sense, *in every period of history, including our own*. The question: "Teacher, what good must I do to have eternal life?" arises in the heart of every individual, and it is Christ alone who is capable of giving the full and definitive answer. The Teacher who expounds God's commandments, who invites others to follow him and gives the grace for a new life, is always present and at work in our midst, as he himself promised: "Lo, I am with you always, to the close of the age" (*Mt* 28:20). *Christ's relevance for people of all times is shown forth in his body, which is the Church.* For this reason the Lord promised his disciples the Holy Spirit, who would "bring to their remembrance" and teach them to understand his commandments (cf. *Jn* 14:26), and who would be the principle and constant course of a new life in the world (cf. *Jn* 3:5–8; *Rom* 8:1–13).

The moral prescriptions which God imparted in the Old Covenant, and which attained their perfection in the New and Eternal Covenant in the very person of the Son of God made man, must be *faithfully kept and continually put into practice* in the various different cultures throughout the course of history. The task of interpreting these prescriptions was entrusted by Jesus to the Apostles and to their successors, with the special assistance of the Spirit of truth: "He who hears you hears me" (*Lk* 10:16). By the light and the strength of this Spirit the Apostles carried out their mission of preaching the Gospel and of pointing out the "way" of the Lord (cf. *Acts* 18:25), teaching above all how to follow and imitate Christ: "For to me to live is Christ" (*Phil* 1:21).

26. In the *moral catechesis of the Apostles*, besides exhortations and directions connected to specific historical and cultural situations, we find an ethical teaching with precise rules of behaviour. This is seen in their Letters, which contain the interpretation, made under the guidance of the Holy Spirit, of the Lord's precepts as they are to be lived in different

---

[34] *In Matthaeum*, Hom. I, 1: PG 57, 15.

cultural circumstances (cf. *Rom* 12—15; *1 Cor* 11—14; *Gal* 5—6; *Eph* 4—6; *Col* 3—4; *1 Pt* and *Jas*). From the Church's beginnings, the Apostles, by virtue of their pastoral responsibility to preach the Gospel, *were vigilant over the right conduct of Christians*,[35] just as they were vigilant for the purity of the faith and the handing down of the divine gifts in the sacraments.[36] The first Christians, coming both from the Jewish people and from the Gentiles, differed from the pagans not only in their faith and their liturgy but also in the witness of their moral conduct, which was inspired by the New Law.[37] The Church is in fact a communion both of faith and of life; her rule of life is "faith working through love" (*Gal* 5:6).

No damage must be done to the *harmony between faith and life: the unity of the Church* is damaged not only by Christians who reject or distort the truths of faith but also by those who disregard the moral obligations to which they are called by the Gospel (cf. *1 Cor* 5:9–13). The Apostles decisively rejected any separation between the commitment of the heart and the actions which express or prove it (cf. *1 Jn* 2:3–6). And ever since Apostolic times the Church's Pastors have unambiguously condemned the behaviour of those who fostered division by their teaching or by their actions.[38]

27. Within the unity of the Church, promoting and preserving the faith and the moral life is the task entrusted by Jesus to the Apostles (cf. *Mt* 28:19–20), a task which continues in the ministry of their successors. This is apparent from the *living Tradition*, whereby—as the Second Vatican Council teaches—"the Church, in her teaching, life and worship, perpetuates and hands on to every generation all that she is and all that she believes. This Tradition which comes from the Apostles, progresses in the Church under the assistance of the Holy Spirit".[39] In the Holy Spirit, the Church receives and hands down the Scripture as the witness to the "great things" which God has done in history (cf. *Lk* 1:49); she professes by the lips of her Fathers and Doctors the truth of the Word made flesh, puts his precepts and love into practice in the lives of her Saints and in the sacrifice of her Martyrs, and celebrates her hope in

---

[35] Cf. SAINT IRENAEUS, *Adversus Haereses*, IV, 26, 2–5: SCh 100/2, 718–729.

[36] Cf. SAINT JUSTIN, *Apologia*, I, 66: PG 6, 427–430.

[37] Cf. *1 Pt* 2: 12 ff.; cf. *Didache*, II, 2: *Patres Apostolici*, ed. F. X. Funk, I, 6–9; CLEMENT OF ALEXANDRIA, *Paedagogus*, I, 10: II, 10: PG 8, 355–364; 497–536; TERTULLIAN, *Apologeticum*, IX, 8: CSEL, 69, 24.

[38] Cf. SAINT IGNATIUS OF ANTIOCH, *Ad Magnesios*, VI, 1–2: *Patres Apostolici*, ed. F. X. Funk, I, 234–235; SAINT IRENAEUS, *Adversus Haereses*, IV, 33: 1, 6, 7: SCh 100/2, 802–805; 814–815; 816–819.

[39] Dogmatic Constitution on Divine Revelation *Dei Verbum*, 8.

the Holy Spirit from heaven on the day of Pentecost, and that the him in the Liturgy. By this same Tradition Christians receive "the living voice of the Gospel",[40] as the faithful expression of God's wisdom and will.

Within Tradition, *the authentic interpretation* of the Lord's law develops, with the help of the Holy Spirit. The same Spirit who is at the origin of the Revelation of Jesus' commandments and teachings guarantees that they will be reverently preserved, faithfully expounded and correctly applied in different times and places. This constant "putting into practice" of the commandments is the sign and fruit of a deeper insight into Revelation and of an understanding in the light of faith of new historical and cultural situations. Nevertheless, it can only confirm the permanent validity of revelation and follow in the line of the interpretation given to it by the great Tradition of the Church's teaching and life, as witnessed by the·teaching of the Fathers, the lives of the Saints, the Church's Liturgy and the teaching of the Magisterium.

In particular, as the Council affirms, "*the task of authentically interpreting the word of God, whether in its written form or in that of Tradition, has been entrusted only to those charged with the Church's living Magisterium, whose authority is exercised in the name of Jesus Christ*".[41] The Church, in her life and teaching, is thus revealed as "the pillar and bulwark of the truth" (*1 Tm* 3:15), including the truth regarding moral action. Indeed, "the Church has the right always and everywhere to proclaim moral principles, even in respect of the social order, and to make judgments about any human matter in so far as this is required by fundamental human rights or the salvation of souls".[42]

Precisely on the questions frequently debated in moral theology today and with regard to which new tendencies and theories have developed, the Magisterium, in fidelity to Jesus Christ and in continuity with the Church's tradition, senses more urgently the duty to offer its own discernment and teaching, in order to help man in his journey towards truth and freedom.

---

[40] Cf. *ibid.*
[41] *Ibid.*, 10.
[42] *Code of Canon Law*, Canon 747, 2.

CHAPTER TWO

"DO NOT BE CONFORMED
TO THIS WORLD"

(Rom 12:2)

THE CHURCH AND THE DISCERNMENT
OF CERTAIN TENDENCIES IN
PRESENT-DAY MORAL THEOLOGY

Teaching what befits sound doctrine (cf. *Tit* 2:1)

28. Our meditation on the dialogue between Jesus and the rich young man has enabled us to bring together the essential elements of revelation in the Old and New Testament with regard to moral action. These are: the *subordination of man and his activity to God*, the One who "alone is good"; the *relationship between the moral good* of human acts *and eternal life; Christian discipleship*, which opens up before man the perspective of perfect love; and finally the *gift of the Holy Spirit*, source and means of the moral life of the "new creation" (cf. *2 Cor* 5:17).

In her reflection on morality, *the Church* has always kept in mind the words of Jesus to the rich young man. Indeed, Sacred Scripture remains the living and fruitful source of the Church's moral doctrine; as the Second Vatican Council recalled, the Gospel is "the source of all saving truth and moral teaching".[43] The Church has faithfully preserved what the word of God teaches, not only about truths which must be believed but also about moral action, action pleasing to God

---

[43] Dogmatic Constitution on Divine Revelation *Dei Verbum*, 7.

(cf. *1 Th* 4:1); she has achieved a *doctrinal development* analogous to that which has taken place in the realm of the truths of faith. Assisted by the Holy Spirit who leads her into all the truth (cf. *Jn* 16:13), the Church has not ceased, nor can she ever cease, to contemplate the "mystery of the Word Incarnate", in whom "light is shed on the mystery of man".[44]

29. The Church's moral reflection, always conducted in the light of Christ, the "Good Teacher", has also developed in the specific form of the theological science called *"moral theology"*, a science which accepts and examines Divine Revelation while at the same time responding to the demands of human reason. Moral theology is a reflection concerned with "morality", with the good and the evil of human acts and of the person who performs them; in this sense it is accessible to all people. But it is also "theology", inasmuch as it acknowledges that the origin and end of moral action are found in the One who "alone is good" and who, by giving himself to man in Christ, offers him the happiness of divine life.

The Second Vatican Council invited scholars to take *"special care for the renewal of moral theology"*, in such a way that "its scientific presentation, increasingly based on the teaching of Scripture, will cast light on the exalted vocation of the faithful in Christ and on their obligation to bear fruit in charity for the life of the world".[45] The Council also encouraged theologians, "while respecting the methods and requirements of theological science, to look for a *more appropriate way of communicating* doctrine to the people of their time; since there is a difference between the deposit or the truths of faith and the manner in which they are expressed, keeping the same meaning and the same judgment".[46] This led to a further invitation, one extended to all the faithful, but addressed to theologians in particular: "The faithful should live in the closest contact with others of their time, and should work for a perfect understanding of their modes of thought and feelings as expressed in their culture".[47]

The work of many theologians who found support in the Council's encouragement has already borne fruit in interesting and helpful reflections about the truths of faith to be believed and applied in life,

---

[44] SECOND VATICAN ECUMENICAL COUNCIL, Pastoral Constitution on the Church in the Modern World *Gaudium et Spes*, 22.

[45] Decree on Priestly Formation *Optatam Totius*, 16.

[46] Pastoral Constitution on the Church in the Modern World *Gaudium et Spes*, 62.

[47] *Ibid.*

reflections offered in a form better suited to the sensitivities and questions of our contemporaries. The Church, and particularly the Bishops, to whom Jesus Christ primarily entrusted the ministry of teaching, are deeply appreciative of this work, and encourage theologians to continue their efforts, inspired by that profound and authentic "fear of the Lord, which is the beginning of wisdom" (cf. *Prov* 1:7).

At the same time, however, within the context of the theological debates which followed the Council, there have developed *certain interpretations of Christian morality which are not consistent with "sound teaching"* (*2 Tm* 4:3). Certainly the Church's Magisterium does not intend to impose upon the faithful any particular theological system, still less a philosophical one. Nevertheless, in order to "reverently preserve and faithfully expound" the word of God,[48] the Magisterium has the duty to state that some trends of theological thinking and certain philosophical affirmations are incompatible with revealed truth.[49]

30. In addressing this Encyclical to you, my Brother Bishops, it is my intention to state *the principles necessary for discerning what is contrary to "sound doctrine"*, drawing attention to those elements of the Church's moral teaching which today appear particularly exposed to error, ambiguity or neglect. Yet these are the very elements on which there depends "the answer to the obscure riddles of the human condition which today also, as in the past, profoundly disturb the human heart. What is man? What is the meaning and purpose of our life? What is good and what is sin? What origin and purpose do sufferings have? What is the way to attaining true happiness? What are death, judgment and retribution after death? Lastly, what is that final, unutterable mystery which embraces our lives and from which we take our origin and towards which we tend?"[50] These and other questions, such as: what is freedom and what is its relationship to the truth contained in God's law? what is the role of conscience in man's moral development? how do we determine, in accordance with the truth about the good, the specific rights and duties of the human person?—can all be summed up in the fundamental question which the young man in the Gospel put to Jesus: "Teacher, what good must I do to have eternal life?"

---

[48] Cf. SECOND VATICAN ECUMENICAL COUNCIL, Dogmatic Constitution on Divine Revelation *Dei Verbum*, 10.

[49] Cf. FIRST VATICAN ECUMENICAL COUNCIL, Dogmatic Constitution of the Catholic Faith *Dei Filius*, Chap. 4: *DS*, 3018.

[50] SECOND VATICAN ECUMENICAL COUNCIL, Declaration on the Relationship of the Church to Non-Christian Religions *Nostra Aetate*, 1.

Because the Church has been sent by Jesus to preach the Gospel and to "make disciples of all nations . . ., teaching them to observe all" that he has commanded (cf. *Mt* 28:19–20), *she today once more puts forward the Master's reply*, a reply that possesses a light and a power capable of answering even the most controversial and complex questions. This light and power also impel the Church constantly to carry out not only her dogmatic but also her moral reflection within an interdisciplinary context, which is especially necessary in facing new issues.[51]

It is in the same light and power that *the Church's Magisterium continues to carry out its task of discernment*, accepting and living out the admonition addressed by the Apostle Paul to Timothy: "I charge you in the presence of God and of Christ Jesus who is to judge the living and the dead, and by his appearing and his kingdom: preach the word, be urgent in season and out of season, convince, rebuke, and exhort, be unfailing in patience and in teaching. For the time will come when people will not endure sound teaching, but having itching ears they will accumulate for themselves teachers to suit their own likings, and will turn away from listening to the truth and wander into myths. As for you, always be steady, endure suffering, do the work of an evangelist, fulfil your ministry" (2 *Tim* 4:1–5; cf. *Tit.* 1:10, 13–14).

"You will know the truth, and the truth will make you free" (*Jn* 8:32)

31. The human issues most frequently debated and differently resolved in contemporary moral reflection are all closely related, albeit in various ways, to a crucial issue: *human freedom.*

Certainly people today have a particularly strong sense of freedom. As the Council's Declaration on Religious Freedom *Dignitatis Humanae* had already observed, "the dignity of the human person is a concern of which people of our time are becoming increasingly more aware".[52] Hence the insistent demand that people be permitted to "enjoy the use of their own responsible judgment and freedom, and decide on their actions

---

[51] Cf. SECOND VATICAN ECUMENICAL COUNCIL, Pastoral Constitution on the Church in the Modern World *Gaudium et Spes*, 43–44.

[52] Declaration on Religious Freedom *Dignitatis Humanae*, 1, referring to JOHN XXIII, Encyclical Letter *Pacem in Terris* (11 April 1963): *AAS* 55 (1963), 279; *ibid.*, 265, and to Pius XII, *Radio Message* (24 December 1944): *AAS* 37 (1945), 14.

on grounds of duty and conscience, without external pressure or coercion".[53] In particular, the right to religious freedom and to respect for conscience on its journey towards the truth is increasingly perceived as the foundation of the cumulative rights of the person.[54]

This heightened sense of the dignity of the human person and of his or her uniqueness, and of the respect due to the journey of conscience, certainly represents one of the positive achievements of modern culture. This perception, authentic as it is, has been expressed in a number of more or less adequate ways, some of which however diverge from the truth about man as a creature and the image of God, and thus need to be corrected and purified in the light of faith.[55]

32.   Certain currents of modern thought have gone so far as to *exalt freedom to such an extent that it becomes an absolute, which would then be the source of values*. This is the direction taken by doctrines which have lost the sense of the transcendent or which are explicitly atheist. The individual conscience is accorded the status of a supreme tribunal of moral judgment which hands down categorical and infallible decisions about good and evil. To the affirmation that one has a duty to follow one's conscience is unduly added the affirmation that one's moral judgment is true merely by the fact that it has its origin in the conscience. But in this way the inescapable claims of truth disappear, yielding their place to a criterion of sincerity, authenticity and "being at peace with oneself", so much so that some have come to adopt a radically subjectivistic conception of moral judgment.

As is immediately evident, *the crisis of truth* is not unconnected with this development. Once the idea of a universal truth about the good, knowable by human reason, is lost, inevitably the notion of conscience also changes. Conscience is no longer considered in its primordial reality as an act of a person's intelligence, the function of which is to apply the universal knowledge of the good in a specific situation and thus to express a judgment about the right conduct to be chosen here and now. Instead, there is a tendency to grant to the individual conscience the prerogative of independently determining the criteria of good and evil

---

[53] Declaration on Religious Freedom *Dignitatis Humanae*, 1.

[54] Cf. Encyclical Letter *Redemptor Hominis* (4 March 1979), 17: *AAS* 71 (1979), 295–300; *Address* To those taking part in the Fifth International Colloquium of Juridical Studies (10 March 1984), 4: *Insegnamenti* VII, 1 (1984), 656; CONGREGATION FOR THE DOCTRINE OF THE FAITH, Instruction on Christian Freedom and Liberation *Libertatis Conscientia* (22 March 1986), 19: *AAS* 79 (1987), 561.

[55] Cf. SECOND VATICAN ECUMENICAL COUNCIL, Pastoral Constitution on the Church in the Modern World *Gaudium et Spes*, 11.

and then acting accordingly. Such an outlook is quite congenial to an individualist ethic, wherein each individual is faced with his own truth, different from the truth of others. Taken to its extreme consequences, this individualism leads to a denial of the very idea of human nature.

These different notions are at the origin of currents of thought which posit a radical opposition between moral law and conscience, and between nature and freedom.

33. *Side by side* with its exaltation of freedom, yet oddly in contrast with it, *modern culture radically questions the very existence of this freedom.* A number of disciplines, grouped under the name of the "behavioural sciences", have rightly drawn attention to the many kinds of psychological and social conditioning which influence the exercise of human freedom. Knowledge of these conditionings and the study they have received represent important achievements which have found application in various areas, for example in pedagogy or the administration of justice. But some people, going beyond the conclusions which can be legitimately drawn from these observations, have come to question or even deny the very reality of human freedom.

Mention should also be made here of theories which misuse scientific research about the human person. Arguing from the great variety of customs, behaviour patterns and institutions present in humanity, these theories end up, if not with an outright denial of universal human values, at least with a relativistic conception of morality.

34. "Teacher, what good must I do to have eternal life?" *The question of morality*, to which Christ provides the answer, *cannot prescind from the issue of freedom. Indeed, it considers that issue central,* for there can be no morality without freedom: "It is only in freedom that man can turn to what is good".[56] *But what sort of freedom?* The Council, considering our contemporaries who "highly regard" freedom and "assiduously pursue" it, but who "often cultivate it in wrong ways as a licence to do anything they please, even evil", speaks of *"genuine" freedom:* 'Genuine freedom is an outstanding manifestation of the divine image in man. For God willed to leave man 'in the power of his own counsel' (cf. *Sir* 15:14), so that he would seek his Creator of his own accord and would freely arrive at full and blessed perfection by cleaving to God'.[57] Although each individual has a right to be respected in his own journey in search of the truth, there exists a prior moral obligation, and a grave one

[56] *Ibid.,* 17.
[57] *Ibid.*

at that, to seek the truth and to adhere to it once it is known.[58] As Cardinal John Henry Newman, that outstanding defender of the rights of conscience, forcefully put it: "Conscience has rights because it has duties".[59]

Certain tendencies in contemporary moral theology, under the influence of the currents of subjectivism and individualism just mentioned, involve novel interpretations of the relationship of freedom to the moral law, human nature and conscience, and propose novel criteria for the moral evaluation of acts. Despite their variety, these tendencies are at one in lessening or even denying *the dependence of freedom on truth.*

If we wish to undertake a critical discernment of these tendencies—a discernment capable of acknowledging which is legitimate, useful and of value in them, while at the same time pointing out their ambiguities, dangers and errors—we must examine them in the light of the fundamental dependence of freedom upon truth, a dependence which has found its clearest and most authoritative expression in the words of Christ: "You will know the truth, and the truth will set you free" (*Jn* 8:32).

I. FREEDOM AND LAW

"Of the tree of the knowledge of good and evil you shall not eat" (*Gen* 2:17)

35. In the Book of Genesis we read: "The Lord God commanded the man, saying, 'You may eat freely of every tree of the garden; but of the tree of the knowledge of good and evil you shall not eat, for in the day that you eat of it you shall die'" (*Gen* 2:16–17).

With this imagery, Revelation teaches that *the power to decide what is good and what is evil does not belong to man, but to God alone.* The man is certainly free, inasmuch as he can understand and accept God's commands. And he possesses an extremely far-reaching freedom, since he can eat "of every tree of the garden". But his freedom is not unlimited: it

---

[58] Cf. SECOND VATICAN ECUMENICAL COUNCIL, Declaration on Religious Freedom *Dignitatis Humanae*, 2; cf. also GREGORY XVI, Encyclical Epistle *Mirari Vos Arbitramur* (15 August 1832): *Acta Gregorii Papae XVI*, I, 169–174; PIUS IX, Encyclical Epistle *Quanta Cura* (8 December 1864): *Pii IX P.M. Acta*, I, 3, 687–700; LEO XIII, Encyclical Letter *Libertas Praestantissimum* (20 June 1888): *Leonis XIII P.M. Acta*, VIII, Romae 1889, 212–246.

[59] *A Letter Addressed to His Grace the Duke of Norfolk: Certain Difficulties Felt by Anglicans in Catholic Teaching* (Uniform Edition: Longman, Green and Company, London, 1868–1881), vol. 2, p. 250.

must halt before the "tree of the knowledge of good and evil", for it is called to accept the moral law given by God. In fact, human freedom finds its authentic and complete fulfilment precisely in the acceptance of that law. God, who alone is good, knows perfectly what is good for man, and by virtue of his very love proposes this good to man in the commandments.

God's law does not reduce, much less do away with human freedom; rather, it protects and promotes that freedom. In contrast, however, some present-day cultural tendencies have given rise to several currents of thought in ethics which centre upon *an alleged conflict between freedom and law*. These doctrines would grant to individuals or social groups the right *to determine what is good or evil*. Human freedom would thus be able to "create values" and would enjoy a primacy over truth, to the point that truth itself would be considered a creation of freedom. Freedom would thus lay claim to a *moral autonomy* which would actually amount to an *absolute sovereignty*.

36. The modern concern for the claims of autonomy has not failed to exercise an *influence* also *in the sphere of Catholic moral theology*. While the latter has certainly never attempted to set human freedom against the divine law or to question the existence of an ultimate religious foundation for moral norms, it has, nonetheless, been led to undertake a profound rethinking about the role of reason and of faith in identifying moral norms with reference to specific "innerworldly" kinds of behaviour involving oneself, others and the material world.

It must be acknowledged that underlying this work of rethinking there are *certain positive concerns* which to a great extent belong to the best tradition of Catholic thought. In response to the encouragement of the Second Vatican Council,[60] there has been a desire to foster dialogue with modern culture, emphasizing the rational—and thus universally understandable and communicable—character of moral norms belonging to the sphere of the natural moral law.[61] There has also been an attempt to reaffirm the interior character of the ethical requirements deriving from that law, requirements which create an obligation for the will only because such an obligation was previously acknowledged by human reason and, concretely, by personal conscience.

Some people, however, disregarding the dependence of human reason on Divine Wisdom and the need, given the present state of fallen nature,

[60] Cf. Pastoral Constitution on the Church in the Modern World *Gaudium et Spes*, 40 and 43.

[61] Cf. SAINT THOMAS AQUINAS, *Summa Theologiae*, I–II, q. 71, a. 6; see also ad 5um.

for Divine Revelation as an effective means for knowing moral truths, even those of the natural order,[62] have actually posited a *complete sovereignty of reason* in the domain of moral norms regarding the right ordering of life in this world. Such norms would constitute the boundaries for a merely "human" morality; they would be the expression of a law which man in an autonomous manner lays down for himself and which has its source exclusively in human reason. In no way could God be considered the Author of this law, except in the sense that human reason exercises its autonomy in setting down laws by virtue of a primordial and total mandate given to man by God. These trends of thought have led to a denial, in opposition to Sacred Scripture (cf. *Mt* 15:3–6) and the Church's constant teaching, of the fact that the natural moral law has God as its author, and that man, by the use of reason, participates in the eternal law, which it is not for him to establish.

37. In their desire, however, to keep the moral life in a Christian context, certain moral theologians have introduced a sharp distinction, contrary to Catholic doctrine,[63] between an *ethical order*, which would be human in origin and of value for *this world* alone, and an *order of salvation*, for which only certain intentions and interior attitudes regarding God and neighbour would be significant. This has then led to an actual denial that there exists, in Divine Revelation, a specific and determined moral content, universally valid and permanent. The word of God would be limited to proposing an exhortation, a generic paraenesis, which the autonomous reason alone would then have the task of completing with normative directives which are truly "objective", that is, adapted to the concrete historical situation. Naturally, an autonomy conceived in this way also involves the denial of a specific doctrinal competence on the part of the Church and her Magisterium with regard to particular moral norms which deal with the so-called "human good". Such norms would not be part of the proper content of Revelation, and would not in themselves be relevant for salvation.

No one can fail to see that such an interpretation of the autonomy of human resolve involves positions incompatible with Catholic teaching.

In such a context it is absolutely necessary to clarify, in the light of the word of God and the living Tradition of the Church, the fundamental notions of human freedom and of the moral law, as well as their profound and intimate relationship. Only thus will it be possible to

---

[62] Cf. Pius XII, Encyclical Letter *Humani Generis* (12 August 1950): *AAS* 42 (1950), 561–562.

[63] Cf. Ecumenical Council of Trent, Sess. VI, Decree on Justification *Cum Hoc Tempore*, Canons 19–21: *DS*, 1569–1571.

respond to the rightful claims of human reason in a way which accepts the valid elements present in certain currents of contemporary moral theology without compromising the Church's heritage of moral teaching with ideas derived from an erroneous concept of autonomy.

"God left man in the power of his own counsel"

(*Sir* 15:14)

38.   Taking up the words of Sirach, the Second Vatican Council explains the meaning of that "genuine freedom" which is "an outstanding manifestation of the divine image" in man: "God willed to leave man in the power of his own counsel, so that he would seek his Creator of his own accord and would freely arrive at full and blessed perfection by cleaving to God".[64] These words indicate the wonderful depth of the *sharing in God's dominion* to which man has been called: they indicate that man's dominion extends in a certain sense over man himself. This has been a constantly recurring theme in theological reflection on human freedom, which is described as a form of kingship. For example, Saint Gregory of Nyssa writes: "The soul shows its royal and exalted character . . . in that it is free and self-governed, swayed autonomously by its own will. Of whom else can this be said, save a king? . . . Thus human nature, created to rule other creatures, was by its likeness to the King of the universe made as it were a living image, partaking with the Archetype both in dignity and in name".[65]

The exercise of dominion over the world represents a great and responsible task for man, one which involves his freedom in obedience to the Creator's command: "Fill the earth and subdue it" (*Gen* 1:28). In view of this, a rightful autonomy is due to every man, as well as to the human community, a fact to which the Council's Constitution *Gaudium et Spes* calls special attention. This is the autonomy of earthly realities, which means that "created things have their own laws and values which are to be gradually discovered, utilized and ordered by man".[66]

39.   Not only the world, however, but also *man himself* has been *entrusted to his own care and responsibility*. God left man "in the power of

---

[64] Pastoral Constitution on the Church in the Modern World *Gaudium et Spes*, 17.

[65] *De Hominis Opificio*, Chap. 4: *PG* 44, 135–136.

[66] Pastoral Constitution on the Church in the Modern World *Gaudium et Spes*, 36.

his own counsel" (*Sir* 15:14), that he might seek his Creator and freely attain perfection. Attaining such perfection means *personally building up that perfection in himself.* Indeed, just as man in exercising his dominion over the world shapes it in accordance with his own intelligence and will, so too in performing morally good acts, man strengthens, develops and consolidates within himself his likeness to God.

Even so, the Council warns against a false concept of the autonomy of earthly realities, one which would maintain that "created things are not dependent on God and that man can use them without reference to their Creator".[67] With regard to man himself, such a concept of autonomy produces particularly baneful effects, and eventually leads to atheism: "Without its Creator the creature simply disappears . . . If God is ignored the creature itself is impoverished".[68]

40. The teaching of the Council emphasizes, on the one hand, *the role of human reason* in discovering and applying the moral law: the moral life calls for that creativity and originality typical of the person, the source and cause of his own deliberate acts. On the other hand, reason draws its own truth and authority from the eternal law, which is none other than divine wisdom itself.[69] At the heart of the moral life we thus find the principle of a "rightful autonomy"[70] of man, the personal subject of his actions. *The moral law has its origin in God and always finds its source in him:* at the same time, by virtue of natural reason, which derives from divine wisdom, it is *a properly human law.* Indeed, as we have seen, the natural law "is nothing other than the light of understanding infused in us by God, whereby we understand what must be done and what must be avoided. God gave this light and this law to man at creation".[71] The rightful autonomy of the practical reason means that man possesses in himself his own law, received from the Creator. Nevertheless, *the autonomy of reason cannot mean* that reason itself *creates values and moral norms.*[72] Were this autonomy to imply a denial of the participation of the practical reason in the wisdom of the divine Creator and Lawgiver, or were it to suggest a freedom which creates moral norms, on the basis

---

[67] *Ibid.*

[68] *Ibid.*

[69] Cf. SAINT THOMAS AQUINAS, *Summa Theologiae*, I–II, q. 93, a. 3, ad 2um, cited by JOHN XXIII, Encyclical Letter *Pacem in Terris* (11 April 1963): *AAS* 55 (1963), 271.

[70] SECOND VATICAN ECUMENICAL COUNCIL, Pastoral Constitution on the Church in the Modern World *Gaudium et Spes*, 41.

[71] SAINT THOMAS AQUINAS, *In Duo Praecepta Caritatis et in Decem Legis Praecepta. Prologus: Opuscula Theologica*, II, No. 1129, Ed. Taurinen. (1954), 245.

[72] Cf. *Address* to a Group of Bishops from the United States on the occasion of their *ad Limina* Visit (15 October 1988), 6: *Insegnamenti*, XI, 3 (1988), 1228.

of historical contingencies or the diversity of societies and cultures, this sort of alleged autonomy would contradict the Church's teaching on the truth about man.[73] It would be the death of true freedom: "But of the tree of the knowledge of good and evil you shall not eat, for in the day that you eat of it you shall die" (*Gen* 2:17).

41.   Man's *genuine moral autonomy* in no way means the rejection but rather the acceptance of the moral law, of God's command: "The Lord God gave this command to the man ..." (*Gen* 2:16). *Human freedom and God's law meet and are called to intersect*, in the sense of man's free obedience to God and of God's completely gratuitous benevolence towards man. Hence obedience to God is not, as some would believe, a *heteronomy*, as if the moral life were subject to the will of something all-powerful, absolute, extraneous to man and intolerant of his freedom. If in fact a heteronomy of morality were to mean a denial of man's self-determination or the imposition of norms unrelated to his good, this would be in contradiction to the Revelation of the Covenant and of the redemptive Incarnation. Such a heteronomy would be nothing but a form of alienation, contrary to divine wisdom and to the dignity of the human person.

Others speak, and rightly so, of *theonomy*, or *participated theonomy*, since man's free obedience to God's law effectively implies that human reason and human will participate in God's wisdom and providence. By forbidding man to "eat of the tree of the knowledge of good and evil", God makes it clear that man does not originally possess such "knowledge" as something properly his own, but only participates in it by the light of natural reason and of Divine Revelation, which manifest to him the requirements and the promptings of eternal wisdom. Law must therefore be considered an expression of divine wisdom: by submitting to the law, freedom submits to the truth of creation. Consequently one must acknowledge in the freedom of the human person the image and nearness of God, who is present in all (cf. *Eph* 4:6). But one must likewise acknowledge the majesty of the God of the universe and revere the holiness of the law of God, who is infinitely transcendent: *Deus semper maior*.[74]

---

[73] Cf. SECOND VATICAN ECUMENICAL COUNCIL, Pastoral Constitution on the Church in the Modern World *Gaudium et Spes*, 47.

[74] Cf. SAINT AUGUSTINE, *Enarratio in Psalmum LXII*, 16: *CCL* 39, 804.

Blessed is the man who takes
delight in the law of the Lord (cf. Ps 1:1–2)

42. Patterned on God's freedom, man's freedom is not negated by his obedience to the divine law; indeed, only through this obedience does it abide in the truth and conform to human dignity. This is clearly stated by the Council: "Human dignity requires man to act through conscious and free choice, as motivated and prompted personally from within, and not through blind internal impulse or merely external pressure. Man achieves such dignity when he frees himself from all subservience to his feelings, and in a free choice of the good, pursues his own end by effectively and assiduously marshalling the appropriate means".[75]

In his journey towards God, the One who "alone is good'", man must freely do good and avoid evil. But in order to accomplish this he must *be able to distinguish good from evil*. And this takes place above all *thanks to the light of natural reason*, the reflection in man of the splendour of God's countenance. Thus Saint Thomas, commenting on a verse of Psalm 4, writes: "After saying: Offer right sacrifices (*Ps* 4:5), as if some had then asked him what right works were, the Psalmist adds: *There are many who say: Who will make us see good?* And in reply to the question he says: *The light of your face, Lord, is signed upon us*, thereby implying that the light of natural reason whereby we discern good from evil, which is the function of the natural law, is nothing else but an imprint on us of the divine light".[76] It also becomes clear why this law is called the natural law: it receives this name not because it refers to the nature of irrational beings but because the reason which promulgates it is proper to human nature.[77]

43. The Second Vatican Council points out that the "supreme rule of life is the divine law itself, the eternal, objective and universal law by which God out of his wisdom and love arranges, directs and governs the whole world and the paths of the human community. God has enabled man to share in this divine law, and hence man is able under the gentle guidance of God's providence increasingly to recognize the unchanging truth".[78]

---

[75] Pastoral Constitution on the Church in the Modern World *Gaudium et Spes*, 17.
[76] *Summa Theologiae*, I–II, q. 91, a. 2.
[77] Cf. *Catechism of the Catholic Church*, No. 1955.
[78] Declaration on Religious Freedom *Dignitatis Humanae*, 3.

The Council refers back to the classic teaching on *God's eternal law*. Saint Augustine defines this as "the reason or the will of God, who commands us to respect the natural order and forbids us to disturb it".[79] Saint Thomas identifies it with "the type of the divine wisdom as moving all things to their due end".[80] And God's wisdom is providence, a love which cares. God himself loves and cares, in the most literal and basic sense, for all creation (cf. *Wis* 7:22; 8:11). But God provides for man differently from the way in which he provides for beings which are not persons. He cares for man not "from without", through the laws of physical nature, but "from within", through reason, which, by its natural knowledge of God's eternal law, is consequently able to show man the right direction to take in his free actions.[81] In this way God calls man to participate in his own providence, since he desires to guide the world—not only the world of nature but also the world of human persons—through man himself, through man's reasonable and responsible care. The *natural law* enters here as the human expression of God's eternal law. Saint Thomas writes: "Among all others, the rational creature is subject to divine providence in the most excellent way, insofar as it partakes of a share of providence, being provident both for itself and for others. Thus it has a share of the Eternal Reason, whereby it has a natural inclination to its proper act and end. This participation of the eternal law in the rational creature is called natural law".[82]

44. The Church has often made reference to the Thomistic doctrine of natural law, including it in her own teaching on morality. Thus my Venerable Predecessor LEO XIII emphasized *the essential subordination of reason and human law to the Wisdom of God and to his law*. After stating that "the *natural law* is written and engraved in the heart of each and every man, since it is none other than human reason itself which commands us to do good and counsels us not to sin", Leo XIII appealed to the "higher reason" of the divine Lawgiver: "But this prescription of human reason could not have the force of law unless it were the voice and the interpreter of some higher reason to which our spirit and our freedom must be subject". Indeed, the force of law consists in its authority to impose duties, to confer rights and to sanction certain behaviour: "Now all of this, clearly, could not exist in man if, as his own supreme legislator, he gave himself the rule of his own actions". And he concluded: "It follows that the natural law is *itself the eternal law*,

---

[79] *Contra Faustum*, Bk 22, Chap. 27: *PL* 42, 418.
[80] *Summa Theologiae*, I–II, q. 93, a. 1.
[81] Cf. *ibid.*, I–II, q. 90, a. 4, ad 1um.
[82] *Ibid.*, I–II, q. 91, a. 2.

implanted in beings endowed with reason, and inclining them *towards their right action and end*; it is none other than the eternal reason of the Creator and Ruler of the universe".[83]

Man is able to recognize good and evil thanks to that discernment of good from evil which he himself carries out by his *reason, in particular by his reason enlightened by Divine Revelation and by faith*, through the law which God gave to the Chosen People, beginning with the commandments on Sinai. Israel was called to accept and to live out *God's law* as *a particular gift and sign of its election and of the divine Covenant,* and also as a pledge of God's blessing. Thus Moses could address the children of Israel and ask them: "What great nation is that that has a god so near to it as the Lord our God is to us, whenever we call upon him? And what great nation is there that has statutes and ordinances so righteous as all this law which I set before you this day?" (*Dt* 4:7–8). In the Psalms we encounter the sentiments of praise, gratitude and veneration which the Chosen People is called to show towards God's law, together with an exhortation to know it, ponder it and translate it into life. "Blessed is the man who walks not in the counsel of the wicked, nor stands in the way of sinners, nor sits in the seat of scoffers, but his delight is in the law of the Lord and on his law he meditates day and night" (*Ps* 1:1–2). "The law of the Lord is perfect, reviving the soul; the testimony of the Lord is sure, making wise the simple; the precepts of the Lord are right, rejoicing the heart; the commandment of the Lord is pure, enlightening the eyes" (*Ps* 18/ 19:8–9).

45. The Church gratefully accepts and lovingly preserves the entire deposit of Revelation, treating it with religious respect and fulfilling her mission of authentically interpreting God's law in the light of the Gospel. In addition, the Church receives the gift of the New Law, which is the "fulfilment" of God's law in Jesus Christ and in his Spirit. This is an "interior" law (cf. *Jer* 31:31–33), "written not with ink but with the Spirit of the living God, not on tablets of stone but on tablets of human hearts" (*2 Cor* 3:3); a law of perfection and of freedom (cf. *2 Cor* 3:17); "the law of the Spirit of life in Christ Jesus" (*Rom* 8:2). Saint Thomas writes that this law "can be called law in two ways. First, the law of the spirit is the Holy Spirit . . . who, dwelling in the soul, not only teaches what it is necessary to do by enlightening the intellect on the things to be done, but also inclines the affections to act with uprightness . . . Second, the law of the spirit can be called the proper effect of the Holy Spirit,

---

[83] Encyclical Letter *Libertas Praestantissimum* (20 June 1888): *Leonis XIII P. M. Acta,* VIII, Romae 1889, 219.

and thus faith working through love (cf. *Gal* 5:6), which teaches inwardly about the things to be done . . . and inclines the affections to act".[84]

Even if moral-theological reflection usually distinguishes between the positive or revealed law of God and the natural law, and, within the economy of salvation, between the "old" and the "new" law, it must not be forgotten that these and other useful distinctions always refer to that law whose author is the one and the same God and which is always meant for man. The different ways in which God, acting in history, cares for the world and for mankind are not mutually exclusive; on the contrary, they support each other and intersect. They have their origin and goal in the eternal, wise and loving counsel whereby God predestines men and women "to be conformed to the image of his Son" (*Rom* 8:29). God's plan poses no threat to man's genuine freedom; on the contrary, the acceptance of God's plan is the only way to affirm that freedom.

"What the law requires is written on their hearts"
(*Rom* 2:15)

46.   The alleged conflict between freedom and law is forcefully brought up once again today with regard to the natural law, and particularly with regard to nature. *Debates about nature and freedom* have always marked the history of moral reflection; they grew especially heated at the time of the Renaissance and the Reformation, as can be seen from the teaching of the Council of Trent.[85] Our own age is marked, though in a different sense, by a similar tension. The penchant for empirical observation, the procedures of scientific objectification, technological progress and certain forms of liberalism have led to these two terms being set in opposition, as if a dialectic, if not an absolute conflict, between freedom and nature were characteristic of the structure of human history. At other periods, it seemed that "nature" subjected man totally to its own dynamics and even its own unbreakable laws. Today too, the situation of the world of the senses within space and time, physio-chemical constants, bodily processes, psychological impulses and forms of social conditioning seem to many people the only really decisive factors of human reality. In this context even moral facts, despite their specificity, are frequently treated as if they were statistically verifiable data, patterns of behaviour which can be subject to observation or

---

[84] *In Epistulam ad Romanos*, c. VIII, lect. 1.
[85] Cf. Sess. IV, Decree on Justification *Cum Hoc Tempore*, Chap. 1: *DS*, 1521.

explained exclusively in categories of psychosocial processes. As a result, *some ethicists*, professionally engaged in the study of human realities and behaviour, can be tempted to take as the standard for their discipline and even for its operative norms the results of a statistical study of concrete human behaviour patterns and the opinions about morality encountered in the majority of people.

Other moralists, however, in their concern to stress the importance of values, remain sensitive to the dignity of freedom, but they frequently conceive of freedom as somehow in opposition to or in conflict with material and biological nature, over which it must progressively assert itself. Here various approaches are at one in overlooking the created dimension of nature and in misunderstanding its integrity. *For some*, "nature" becomes reduced to raw material for human activity and for its power: thus nature needs to be profoundly transformed, and indeed overcome by freedom, inasmuch as it represents a limitation and denial of freedom. *For others*, it is in the untrammelled advancement of man's power, or of his freedom, that economic, cultural, social and even moral values are established: nature would thus come to mean everything found in man and the world apart from freedom. In such an understanding, nature would include in the first place the human body, its make-up and its processes: against this physical datum would be opposed whatever is "constructed", in other words "culture", seen as the product and result of freedom. Human nature, understood in this way, could be reduced to and treated as a readily available biological or social material. This ultimately means making freedom self-defining and a phenomenon creative of itself and its values. Indeed, when all is said and done man would not even have a nature; he would be his own personal life-project. Man would be nothing more than his own freedom!

47. In this context, *objections of physicalism and naturalism* have been levelled against the traditional conception of *the natural law*, which is accused of presenting as moral laws what are in themselves mere biological laws. Consequently, in too superficial a way, a permanent and unchanging character would be attributed to certain kinds of human behaviour, and, on the basis of this, an attempt would be made to formulate universally valid moral norms. According to certain theologians, this kind of "biologistic or naturalistic argumentation" would even be present in certain documents of the Church's Magisterium, particularly those dealing with the area of sexual and conjugal ethics. It was, they maintain, on the basis of a naturalistic understanding of the sexual act that contraception, direct sterilization, autoeroticism, pre-marital sexual relations, homosexual relations and artificial insemination were condemned as morally unacceptable. In the opinion of these same theologians, a morally negative evaluation of such acts fails to take into adequate consideration both man's character as a rational and free being and the cultural conditioning of all moral norms. In their view, man, as a rational being, not only can but actually *must freely determine the meaning* of his behaviour. This process of "determining the meaning" would obviously have to take into account the many limitations of the human being, as existing in a body and in history. Furthermore, it would have to take into consideration the behavioural models and the meanings which the latter acquire in any given culture. Above all, it would have to respect the fundamental commandment of love of God and neighbour. Still, they continue, God made man as a rationally free being; he left him "in the power of his own counsel" and he expects him to shape his life in a personal and rational way. Love of neighbour would mean above all and even exclusively respect for his freedom to make his own decisions. The workings of typically human behaviour, as well as the so-called "natural inclinations", would establish at the most—so they say—a general orientation towards correct behaviour, but they cannot determine the moral assessment of individual human acts, so complex from the viewpoint of situations.

48. Faced with this theory, one has to consider carefully the correct relationship existing between freedom and human nature, and in particular *the place of the human body in questions of natural law.*

A freedom which claims to be absolute ends up treating the human body as a raw datum, devoid of any meaning and moral values until freedom has shaped it in accordance with its design. Consequently, human nature and the body appear as *presuppositions or preambles*, materially *necessary* for freedom to make its choice, yet extrinsic to the person, the subject and the human act. Their functions would not be able to constitute reference points for moral decisions, because the finalities of these inclinations would be merely "*physical*" goods, called by some "pre-moral". To refer to them, in order to find in them rational indications with regard to the order of morality, would be to expose oneself to the accusation of physicalism or biologism. In this way of thinking, the tension between freedom and a nature conceived of in a reductive way is resolved by a division within man himself.

This moral theory does not correspond to the truth about man and his freedom. It contradicts the *Church's teachings on the unity of the human person,* whose rational soul is *per se et essentialiter* the form of his body.[86] The spiritual and immortal soul is the principle of unity of the human

---

[86] Cf. ECUMENICAL COUNCIL OF VIENNE, Constitution *Fidei Catholicae: DS,* 902; FIFTH LATERAN ECUMENICAL COUNCIL, Bull *Apostolici Regiminis: DS,* 1440.

being, whereby it exists as a whole—*corpore et anima unus*[87]—as a person. These definitions not only point out that the body, which has been promised the resurrection, will also share in glory. They also remind us that reason and free will are linked with all the bodily and sense faculties. *The person, including the body, is completely entrusted to himself, and it is in the unity of body and soul that the person is the subject of his own moral acts.* The person, by the light of reason and the support of virtue, discovers in the body the anticipatory signs, the expression and the promise of the gift of self, in conformity with the wise plan of the Creator. It is in the light of the dignity of the human person—a dignity which must be affirmed for its own sake—that reason grasps the specific moral value of certain goods towards which the person is naturally inclined. And since the human person cannot be reduced to a freedom which is self-designing, but entails a particular spiritual and bodily structure, the primordial moral requirement of loving and respecting the person as an end and never as a mere means also implies, by its very nature, respect for certain fundamental goods, without which one would fall into relativism and arbitrariness.

49. *A doctrine which dissociates the moral act from the bodily dimensions of its exercise is contrary to the teaching of Scripture and Tradition.* Such a doctrine revives, in new forms, certain ancient errors which have always been opposed by the Church, inasmuch as they reduce the human person to a "spiritual" and purely formal freedom. This reduction misunderstands the moral meaning of the body and of kinds of behaviour involving it (cf. *1 Cor* 6:19). Saint Paul declares that "the immoral, idolaters, adulterers, sexual perverts, thieves, the greedy, drunkards, revilers, robbers" are excluded from the Kingdom of God (cf. *1 Cor* 6:9). This condemnation—repeated by the Council of Trent"[88]—lists as "mortal sins" or "immoral practices" certain specific kinds of behaviour the willful acceptance of which prevents believers from sharing in the inheritance promised to them. In fact, *body and soul are inseparable:* in the person, in the willing agent and in the deliberate act, *they stand or fall together.*

50. At this point the true meaning of the natural law can be

---

[87] Second Vatican Ecumenical Council Pastoral Constitution on the Church in the Modern World *Gaudium et Spes*, 14.

[88] Cf. Sess. VI, Decree on Justification *Cum Hoc Tempore*, Chap. 15: *DS*, 1544. The Post-Synodal Apostolic Exhortation on Reconciliation and Penance in the Mission of the Church Today cites other texts of the Old and New Testaments which condemn as mortal sins certain modes of conduct involving the body: cf. *Reconciliatio et Paenitentia* (2 December 1984), 17: *AAS* 77 (1985), 218–223.

understood: it refers to man's proper and primordial nature, the "nature of the human person",[89] which is *the person himself in the unity of soul and body*, in the unity of his spiritual and biological inclinations and of all the other specific characteristics necessary for the pursuit of his end. "The natural moral law expresses and lays down the purposes, rights and duties which are based upon the bodily and spiritual nature of the human person. Therefore this law cannot be thought of as simply a set of norms on the biological level; rather it must be defined as the rational order whereby man is called by the Creator to direct and regulate his life and actions and in particular to make use of his own body".[90] To give an example, the origin and the foundation of the duty of absolute respect for human life are to be found in the dignity proper to the person and not simply in the natural inclination to preserve one's own physical life. Human life, even though it is a fundamental good of man, thus acquires a moral significance in reference to the good of the person, who must always be affirmed for his own sake. While it is always morally illicit to kill an innocent human being, it can be licit, praiseworthy or even imperative to give up one's own life (cf. *Jn* 15:13) out of love of neighbour or as a witness to the truth. Only in reference to the human person in his "unified totality", that is, as "a soul which expresses itself in a body and a body informed by an immortal spirit",[91] can the specifically human meaning of the body be grasped. Indeed, natural inclinations take on moral relevance only insofar as they refer to the human person and his authentic fulfilment, a fulfilment which for that matter can take place always and only in human nature. By rejecting all manipulations of corporeity which alter its human meaning, the Church serves man and shows him the path of true love, the only path on which he can find the true God.

The natural law thus understood does not allow for any division between freedom and nature. Indeed, these two realities are harmoniously bound together, and each is intimately linked to the other.

[89] SECOND VATICAN ECUMENICAL COUNCIL, Pastoral Constitution on the Church in the Modern World *Gaudium et Spes*, 51.
[90] CONGREGATION FOR THE DOCTRINE OF THE FAITH, Instruction on Respect for Human Life in its Origin and on the Dignity of Procreation *Donum Vitae* (22 February 1987), Introduction, 3: *AAS* 80 (1988), 74; cf. PAUL VI, Encyclical Letter *Humanae Vitae* (25 July 1968), 10: *AAS* 60 (1868), 487-488.
[91] Apostolic Exhortation *Familiaris Consortio* (22 November 1981), 11: *AAS* 74 (1982), 92.

"From the beginning it was not so" (*Mt* 19:8)

51. The alleged conflict between freedom and nature also has repercussions on the interpretation of certain specific aspects of the natural law, especially its *universality and immutability*. "Where then are these rules written", Saint Augustine wondered, "except in the book of that light which is called truth? From thence every just law is transcribed and transferred to the heart of the man who works justice, not by wandering but by being, as it were, impressed upon it, just as the image from the ring passes over to the wax, and yet does not leave the ring".[92]

Precisely because of this "truth" *the natural law involves universality*. Inasmuch as it is inscribed in the rational nature of the person, it makes itself felt to all beings endowed with reason and living in history. In order to perfect himself in his specific order, the person must do good and avoid evil, be concerned for the transmission and preservation of life, refine and develop the riches of the material world, cultivate social life, seek truth, practise good and contemplate beauty.[93]

The separation which some have posited between the freedom of individuals and the nature which all have in common, as it emerges from certain philosophical theories which are highly influential in present-day culture, obscures the perception of the universality of the moral law on the part of reason. But inasmuch as the natural law expresses the dignity of the human person and lays the foundation for his fundamental rights and duties, it is universal in its precepts and its authority extends to all mankind. *This universality does not ignore the individuality of human beings*, nor is it opposed to the absolute uniqueness of each person. On the contrary, it embraces as its root each of the person's free acts, which are meant to bear witness to the universality of the true good. By submitting to the common law, our acts build up the true communion of persons and, by God's grace, practise charity, "which binds everything together in perfect harmony" (*Col* 3:14). When on the contrary they disregard the law, or even are merely ignorant of it, whether culpably or not, our acts damage the communion of persons, to the detriment of each.

52. It is right and just, always and for everyone, to serve God, to render him the worship which is his due and to honour one's parents as they deserve. Positive precepts such as these, which order us to perform certain actions and to cultivate certain dispositions, are universally binding;

---

[92] *De Trinitate*, XIV, 15, 21: CCL 50/A, 451.
[93] Cf. Saint Thomas Aquinas, *Summa Theologiae*, I–II, q. 94, a. 2.

they are "unchanging".[94] They unite in the same common good all people of every period of history, created for "the same divine calling and destiny".[95] These universal and permanent laws correspond to things known by the practical reason and are applied to particular acts through the judgment of conscience. The acting subject personally assimilates the truth contained in the law. He appropriates this truth of his being and makes it his own by his acts and the corresponding virtues. The *negative precepts* of the natural law are universally valid. They oblige each and every individual, always and in every circumstance. It is a matter of prohibitions which forbid a given action *semper et pro semper*, without exception, because the choice of this kind of behaviour is in no case compatible with the goodness of the will of the acting person, with his vocation to life with God and to communion with his neighbour. It is prohibited—to everyone and in every case—to violate these precepts. They oblige everyone, regardless of the cost, never to offend in anyone, beginning with oneself, the personal dignity common to all.

On the other hand, the fact that only the negative commandments oblige always and under all circumstances does not mean that in the moral life prohibitions are more important than the obligation to do good indicated by the positive commandments. The reason is this: the commandment of love of God and neighbour does not have in its dynamic any higher limit, but it does have a lower limit, beneath which the commandment is broken. Furthermore, what must be done in any given situation depends on the circumstances, not all of which can be foreseen; on the other hand there are kinds of behaviour which can never, in any situation, be a proper response—a response which is in conformity with the dignity of the person. Finally, it is always possible that man, as the result of coercion or other circumstances, can be hindered from doing certain good actions; but he can never be hindered from not doing certain actions, especially if he is prepared to die rather than to do evil.

The Church has always taught that one may never choose kinds of behaviour prohibited by the moral commandments expressed in negative

---

[94] Cf. Second Vatican Ecumenical Council, Pastoral Constitution on the Church in the Modern World *Gaudium et Spes*, 10; Sacred Congregation for the Doctrine of the Faith, Declaration on Certain Questions concerning Sexual Ethics *Persona Humana* (29 December 1975), 4: *AAS* 68 (1976), 80: "But in fact, divine Revelation and, in its own proper order, philosophical wisdom, emphasize the authentic exigencies of human nature. They thereby necessarily manifest the existence of immutable laws inscribed in the constitutive elements of human nature and which are revealed to be identical in all beings endowed with reason".

[95] Second Vatican Ecumenical Council, Pastoral Constitution on the Church in the Modern World *Gaudium et Spes*, 29.

form in the Old and New Testaments. As we have seen, Jesus himself reaffirms that these prohibitions allow no exceptions: "If you wish to enter into life, keep the commandments . . . You shall not murder, You shall not commit adultery, You shall not steal, You shall not bear false witness" (*Mt* 19:17–18).

53. The great concern of our contemporaries for historicity and for culture has led some to call into question *the immutability of the natural law* itself, and thus the existence of "objective norms of morality"[96] valid for all people of the present and the future, as for those of the past. Is it ever possible, they ask, to consider as universally valid and always binding certain rational determinations established in the past, when no one knew the progress humanity would make in the future?

It must certainly be admitted that man always exists in a particular culture, but it must also be admitted that man is not exhaustively defined by that same culture. Moreover, the very progress of cultures demonstrates that there is something in man which transcends those cultures. This "something" is precisely human nature: this nature is itself the measure of culture and the condition ensuring that man does not become the prisoner of any of his cultures, but asserts his personal dignity by living in accordance with the profound truth of his being. To call into question the permanent structural elements of man which are connected with his own bodily dimension would not only conflict with common experience, but would render meaningless *Jesus' reference to the "beginning"*, precisely where the social and cultural context of the time had distorted the primordial meaning and the role of certain moral norms (cf. *Mt* 19:1–9). This is the reason why "the Church affirms that underlying so many changes there are some things which do not change and are *ultimately founded upon Christ*, who is the same yesterday and today and for ever".[97] Christ is the "Beginning" who, having taken on human nature, definitively illumines it in its constitutive elements and in its dynamism of charity towards God and neighbour.[98]

Certainly there is a need to seek out and to discover *the most adequate formulation* for universal and permanent moral norms in the light of different cultural contexts, a formulation most capable of ceaselessly

[96] Cf. *ibid.*, 16.
[97] *Ibid.*, 10.
[98] Cf. SAINT THOMAS AQUINAS, *Summa Theologiae* I–II, q. 108, a. 1. St Thomas bases the fact that mortal norms, even in the context of the New Law, are not merely formal in character but have a determined content, upon the assumption of human nature by the Word.

expressing their historical relevance, of making them understood and of authentically interpreting their truth. This truth of the moral law—like that of the "deposit of faith"—unfolds down the centuries: the norms expressing that truth remain valid in their substance, but must be specified and determined *"eodem sensu eademque sententia"*[99] in the light of historical circumstances by the Church's Magisterium, whose decision is preceded and accompanied by the work of interpretation and formulation characteristic of the reason of individual believers and of theological reflection.[100]

II CONSCIENCE AND TRUTH

Man's sanctuary

54.   The relationship between man's freedom and God's law is most deeply lived out in the "heart" of the person, in his moral conscience. As the Second Vatican Council observed: "In the depths of his conscience man detects a law which he does not impose on himself, but which holds him to obedience. Always summoning him to love good and avoid evil, the voice of conscience can when necessary speak to his heart more specifically: 'do this, shun that'. For man has in his heart a law written by God. To obey it is the very dignity of man; according to it he will be judged (cf. *Rom* 2:14–16)".[101]

The way in which one conceives the relationship between freedom and law is thus intimately bound up with one's understanding of the moral conscience. Here the cultural tendencies referred to above—in which freedom and law are set in opposition to each another and kept apart, and freedom is exalted almost to the point of idolatry—lead to a *"creative" understanding of moral conscience*, which diverges from the teaching of the Church's tradition and her Magisterium.

[99] SAINT VINCENT OF LERINS, Commonitorium Primum, c. 23: *PL* 50, 668.

[100] The development of the Church's moral doctrine is similar to that of the doctrine of the faith (cf. FIRST VATICAN ECUMENICAL COUNCIL, Dogmatic Constitution on the Catholic Faith *Dei Filius*, Chap. 4: *DS*, 3020, and Canon 4: *DS*, 3024). The words spoken by JOHN XXIII at the opening of the Second Vatican Council can also be applied to moral doctrine: "This certain and unchanging teaching (i.e., Christian doctrine in its completeness), to which the faithful owe obedience, needs to be more deeply understood and set forth in a way adapted to the needs of our time. Indeed, this deposit of the faith, the truths contained in our time-honoured teaching, is one thing; the manner in which these truths are set forth (with their meaning preserved intact) is something else": *AAS* 54 (1962), 792; cf. *L'Osservatore Romano*, 12 October 1962, p. 2.

[101] Pastoral Constitution on the Church in the Modern World *Gaudium et Spes*, 16.

55. According to the opinion of some theologians, the function of conscience had been reduced, at least at a certain period in the past, to a simple application of general moral norms to individual cases in the life of the person. But those norms, they continue, cannot be expected to foresee and to respect all the individual concrete acts of the person in all their uniqueness and particularity. While such norms might somehow be useful for a correct *assessment* of the situation, they cannot replace the individual personal *decision* on how to act in particular cases. The critique already mentioned of the traditional understanding of human nature and of its importance for the moral life has even led certain authors to state that these norms are not so much a binding objective criterion for judgments of conscience, but a *general perspective* which helps man tentatively to put order into his personal and social life. These authors also stress the *complexity* typical of the phenomenon of conscience, a complexity profoundly related to the whole sphere of psychology and the emotions, and to the numerous influences exerted by the individual's social and cultural environment. On the other hand, they give maximum attention to the value of conscience, which the Council itself defined as "the sanctuary of man, where he is alone with God whose voice echoes within him".[102] This voice, it is said, leads man not so much to a meticulous observance of universal norms as to a creative and responsible acceptance of the personal tasks entrusted to him by God.

In their desire to emphasize the "creative" character of conscience, certain authors no longer call its actions "judgments" but "decisions": only by making these decisions "autonomously" would man be able to attain moral maturity. Some even hold that this process of maturing is inhibited by the excessively categorical position adopted by the Church's Magisterium in many moral questions; for them, the Church's interventions are the cause of unnecessary *conflicts of conscience*.

56. In order to justify these positions, some authors have proposed a kind of double status of moral truth. Beyond the doctrinal and abstract level, one would have to acknowledge the priority of a certain more concrete existential consideration. The latter, by taking account of circumstances and the situation, could legitimately be the basis of certain *exceptions to the general rule* and thus permit one to do in practice and in good conscience what is qualified as intrinsically evil by the moral law. A separation, or even an opposition, is thus established in some cases between the teaching of the precept, which is valid in general, and the norm of the individual conscience, which would in fact make the final decision about what is good and what is evil. On this basis, an attempt is

---

[102] *Ibid.*

made to legitimize so-called "pastoral" solutions contrary to the teaching of the Magisterium, and to justify a "creative" hermeneutic according to which the moral conscience is in no way obliged, in every case, by a particular negative precept.

No one can fail to realize that these approaches post a challenge to the *very identity of the moral conscience* in relation to human freedom and God's law. Only the clarification made earlier with regard to the relationship, based on truth, between freedom and law makes possible a *discernment* concerning this "creative" understanding of conscience.

The judgment of conscience

57. The text of the Letter to the Romans which has helped us to grasp the essence of the natural law also indicates *the biblical understanding of conscience*, especially *in its specific connection with the law:* "When Gentiles who have not the law do by nature what the law requires, they are a law unto themselves, even though they do not have the law. They show that what the law requires is written on their hearts, while their conscience also bears witness and their conflicting thoughts accuse or perhaps excuse them" (*Rom* 2:14–15).

According to Saint Paul, conscience in a certain sense confronts man with the law, and thus becomes a *"witness" for man:* a witness of his own faithfulness or unfaithfulness with regard to the law, of his essential moral rectitude or iniquity. Conscience is the *only* witness, since what takes place in the heart of the person is hidden from the eyes of everyone outside. Conscience makes its witness known only to the person himself. And, in turn, only the person himself knows what his own response is to the voice of conscience.

58. The importance of this interior *dialogue of man with himself* can never be adequately appreciated. But it is also a *dialogue of man with God*, the author of the law, the primordial image and final end of man. Saint Bonaventure teaches that "conscience is like God's herald and messenger; it does not command things on its own authority, but commands them as coming from God's authority, like a herald when he proclaims the edict of the king. This is why conscience has binding force".[103] Thus it can be said that conscience bears witness to man's own rectitude or iniquity to man himself but, together with this and indeed even before-hand, conscience is *the witness of God himself*, whose voice and judgment

---

[103] *In II Librum Sentent.*, dist. 39, a. 1, q. 3, conclusion: Ed. Ad Claras Aquas, II, 907b.

penetrate the depths of man's soul, calling him *fortiter et suaviter* to obedience. "Moral conscience does not close man within an insurmountable and impenetrable solitude, but opens him to the call, to the voice of God. In this, and not in anything else, lies the entire mystery and the dingity of the moral conscience: in being the place, the sacred place where God speaks to man".[104]

59.   Saint Paul does not merely acknowledge that conscience acts as a "witness"; he also reveals the way in which conscience performs that function. He speaks of "conflicting thoughts" which accuse or excuse the Gentiles with regard to their behaviour (cf. *Rom* 2:15). The term "conflicting thoughts" clarifies the precise nature of conscience: it is a *moral judgment about man and his actions*, a judgment either of acquittal or of condemnation, according as human acts are in conformity or not with the law of God written on the heart. In the same text the Apostle clearly speaks of the judgment of actions, the judgment of their author and the moment when that judgment will be definitively rendered: "(This will take place) on that day when, according to my Gospel, God judges the secrets of men by Christ Jesus" (*Rom* 2:16).

The judgment of conscience is a *practical judgment*, a judgment which makes known what man must do or not do, or which assesses an act already performed by him. It is a judgment which applies to a concrete situation the rational conviction that one must love and do good and avoid evil. This first principle of practical reason is part of the natural law; indeed it constitutes the very foundation of the natural law, inasmuch as it expresses that primordial insight about good and evil, that reflection of God's creative wisdom which, like an imperishable spark (*scintilla animae*), shines in the heart of every man. But whereas the natural law discloses the objective and universal demands of the moral good, conscience is the application of the law to a particular case; this application of the law thus becomes an inner dictate for the individual, a summons to do what is good in this particular situation. Conscience thus formulates *moral obligation* in the light of the natural law: it is the obligation to do what the individual, through the workings of his conscience, *knows* to be a good he is called to do *here and now*. The universality of the law and its obligation are acknowledged, not suppressed, once reason has established the law's application in concrete present circumstances. The judgment of conscience states "in an ultimate way" whether a certain particular kind of behaviour is in conformity with the law; it formulates the proximate

---

[104] *Address* (General Audience, 17 August 1983), 2: *Insegnamenti*, VI, 2 (1983), 256.

norm of the morality of a voluntary act, "applying the objective law to a particular case".[105]

60.   Like the natural law itself and all practical knowledge, the judgment of conscience also has an imperative character: man must act in accordance with it. If man acts against this judgment or, in a case where he lacks certainty about the rightness and goodness of a determined act, still performs that act, he stands condemned by his own conscience, *the proximate norm of personal morality.* The dignity of this rational forum and the authority of its voice and judgments derive from the *truth* about moral good and evil, which it is called to listen to and to express. This truth is indicated by the "divine law", *the universal and objective norm of morality.* The judgment of conscience does not establish the law; rather it bears witness to the authority of the natural law and of the practical reason with reference to the supreme good, whose attractiveness the human person perceives and whose commandments he accepts. "Conscience is not an independent and exclusive capacity to decide what is good and what is evil. Rather there is profoundly imprinted upon it a principle of obedience vis-à-vis the objective norm which establishes and conditions the correspondence of its decisions with the commands and prohibitions which are at the basis of human behaviour".[106]

61.   The truth about moral good, as that truth is declared in the law of reason, is practically and concretely recognized by the judgment of conscience, which leads one to take responsibility for the good or the evil one has done. If man does evil, the just judgment of his conscience remains within him as a witness to the universal truth of the good, as well as to the malice of his particular choice. But the verdict of conscience remains in him also as a pledge of hope and mercy: while bearing witness to the evil he has done, it also reminds him of his need, with the help of God's grace, to ask forgiveness, to do good and to cultivate virtue constantly.

Consequently *in the practical judgment of conscience,* which imposes on the person the obligation to perform a given act, *the link between freedom and truth is made manifest.* Precisely for this reason conscience expresses itself in acts of "judgment" which reflect the truth about the good, and

---

[105] Supreme Sacred Congregation of the Holy Office, Instruction on "Situation Ethics" *Contra Doctrinam* (2 February 1956): *AAS* 48 (1956), 144.

[106] Encyclical Letter *Dominum et Vivificantem* (18 May 1986), 43: *AAS* 78 (1986), 859; cf. Second Vatican Ecumenical Council, Pastoral Constitution on the Church in the Modern World *Gaudium et Spes*, 16; Declaration on Religious Freedom *Dignitatis Humanae*, 3.

not in arbitrary "decisions". The maturity and responsibility of these judgments—and, when all is said and done, of the individual who is their subject—are not measured by the liberation of the conscience from objective truth, in favour of an alleged autonomy in personal decisions, but, on the contrary, by an insistent search for truth and by allowing oneself to be guided by that truth in one's actions.

Seeking what is true and good

62.   Conscience, as the judgment of an act, is not exempt from the possibility of error. As the Council puts it, "not infrequently conscience can be mistaken as a result of invincible ignorance, although it does not on that account forfeit its dignity; but this cannot be said when a man shows little concern for seeking what is true and good, and conscience gradually becomes almost blind from being accustomed to sin".[107] In these brief words the Council sums up the doctrine which the Church down the centuries has developed with regard to the *erroneous conscience*.

Certainly, in order to have a "good conscience" (*1 Tim* 1:5), man must seek the truth and must make judgments in accordance with that same truth. As the Apostle Paul says, the conscience must be "confirmed by the Holy Spirit" (cf. *Rom* 9:1); it must be "clear" (*2 Tim* 1:3); it must not "practise cunning and tamper with God's word", but "openly state the truth" (cf. *2 Cor* 4:2). On the other hand, the Apostle also warns Christians: "Do not be conformed to this world but be transformed by the renewal of your mind, that you may prove what is the will of God, what is good and acceptable and perfect" (*Rom* 12:2).

Paul's admonition urges us to be watchful, warning us that in the judgments of our conscience the possibility of error is always present. Conscience *is not an infallible judge;* it can make mistakes. However, error of conscience can be the result of an *invincible ignorance*, an ignorance of which the subject is not aware and which he is unable to overcome by himself.

The Council reminds us that in cases where such invincible ignorance is not culpable, conscience does not lose its dignity, because even when it directs us to act in a way not in conformity with the objective moral order, it continues to speak in the name of that truth about the good which the subject is called to seek sincerely.

63.   In any event, it is always from the truth that the dignity of

---

[107] SECOND VATICAN ECUMENICAL COUNCIL, Pastoral Constitution on the Church in the Modern World *Gaudium et Spes*, 16.

conscience derives. In the case of the correct conscience, it is a question of the *objective truth* received by man; in the case of the erroneous conscience, it is a question of what man, mistakenly, *subjectively* considers to be true. It is never acceptable to confuse a "subjective" error about moral good with the "objective" truth rationally proposed to man in virtue of his end, or to make the moral value of an act performed with a true and correct conscience equivalent to the moral value of an act performed by following the judgment of an erroneous conscience.[108] It is possible that the evil done as the result of invincible ignorance or a non-culpable error of judgment may not be imputable to the agent; but even in this case it does not cease to be an evil, a disorder in relation to the truth about the good. Furthermore, a good act which is not recognized as such does not contribute to the moral growth of the person who performs it; it does not perfect him and it does not help to dispose him for the supreme good. Thus, before feeling easily justified in the name of our conscience, we should reflect on the words of the Psalm: "Who can discern his errors? Clear me from hidden faults" (*Ps* 19:12). There are faults which we fail to see but which nevertheless remain faults, because we have refused to walk towards the light (cf. *Jn* 9:39–41).

Conscience, as the ultimate concrete judgment, compromises its dignity when it is *culpably erroneous*, that is to say, "when man shows little concern for seeking what is true and good, and conscience gradually becomes almost blind from being accustomed to sin".[109] Jesus alludes to the danger of the conscience being formed when he warns: "The eye is the lamp of the body. So if your eye is sound, your whole body will be full of light; but if your eye is not sound, your whole body will be full of darkness. If then the light in you is darkness, how great is the darkness!" (*Mt* 6:22–23).

64.   The words of Jesus just quoted also represent a call to *form our conscience*, to make it the object of a continuous conversion to what is true and to what is good. In the same vein, Saint Paul exhorts us not to be conformed to the mentality of this world, but to be transformed by the renewal of our mind (cf. *Rom* 12:2). It is the "heart" converted to the Lord and to the love of what is good which is really the source of *true* judgments of conscience. Indeed, in order to "prove what is the will of God, what is good and acceptable and perfect" (*Rom* 12:2), knowledge of God's law in general is certainly necessary, but it is not sufficient: what

---

[108] Cf. SAINT THOMAS AQUINAS, *De Veritate*, q. 17, a. 4.

[109] SECOND VATICAN ECUMENICAL COUNCIL, Pastoral Constitution on the Church in the Modern World *Gaudium et Spes*, 16.

is essential is a sort of *"connaturality"* between man and the true good.[110] Such a connaturality is rooted in and develops through the virtuous attitudes of the individual himself: prudence and the other cardinal virtues, and even before these the theological virtues of faith, hope and charity. This is the meaning of Jesus' saying: "He who does what is true comes to the light" (*Jn* 3:21).

Christians have a great help for the formation of conscience *in the Church and her Magisterium*. As the Council affirms: "In forming their consciences the Christian faithful must give careful attention to the sacred and certain teaching of the Church. For the Catholic Church is by the will of Christ the teacher of truth. Her charge is to announce and teach authentically that truth which is Christ, and at the same time with her authority to declare and confirm the principles of the moral order which derive from human nature itself".[111] It follows that the authority of the Church, when she pronounces on moral questions, in no way undermines the freedom of conscience of Christians. This is so not only because freedom of conscience is never freedom "from" the truth but always and only freedom "in" the truth, but also because the Magisterium does not bring to the Christian conscience truths which are extraneous to it; rather it brings to light the truths which it ought already to possess, developing them from the starting point of the primordial act of faith. The Church puts herself always and only at the *service of conscience*, helping it to avoid being tossed to and fro by every wind of doctrine proposed by human deceit (cf. *Eph* 4:14), and helping it not to swerve from the truth about the good of man, but rather, especially in more difficult questions, to attain the truth with certainty and to abide in it.

III. FUNDAMENTAL CHOICE AND SPECIFIC KINDS OF BEHAVIOUR

"Only do not use your freedom as an opportunity for the flesh" (*Gal* 5:13)

65. The heightened concern for freedom in our own day has led many students of the behavioural and the theological sciences to develop a more penetrating analysis of its nature and of its dynamics. It has been

---

[110] Cf. Saint Thomas Aquinas, *Summa Theologiae*, II–II, q. 45, a. 2.
[111] Declaration on Religious Freedom *Dignitatis Humanae*, 14.

rightly pointed out that freedom is not only the choice for one or another particular action; it is also, within that choice, a *decision about oneself* and a setting of one's own life for or against the Good, for or against the Truth, and ultimately for or against God. Emphasis has rightly been placed on the importance of certain choices which "shape" a person's entire moral life, and which serve as bounds within which other particular everyday choices can be situated and allowed to develop.

Some authors, however, have proposed an even more radical revision of the *relationship between person and acts*. They speak of a "fundamental freedom", deeper than and different from freedom of choice, which needs to be considered if human actions are to be correctly understood and evaluated. According to these authors, the *key role in the moral life* is to be attributed to a "fundamental option", brought about by that fundamental freedom whereby the person makes an overall self-determination, not through a specific and conscious decision on the level of reflection, but in a "transcendental" and "athematic" way. *Particular acts* which flow from this option would constitute only partial and never definitive attempts to give it expression; they would only be its "signs" or symptoms. The immediate object of such acts would not be absolute Good (before which the freedom of the person would be expressed on a transcendental level), but particular (also termed "categorical") goods. In the opinion of some theologians, none of these goods, which by their nature are partial, could determine the freedom of man as a person in his totality, even though it is only by bringing them about or refusing to do so that man is able to express his own fundamental option.

A *distinction* thus comes to be introduced *between the fundamental option and deliberate choices of a concrete kind of behaviour*. In some authors this division tends to become a *separation*, when they expressly limit moral "good" and "evil" to the transcendental dimension proper to the fundamental option, and describe as "right" or "wrong" the choices of particular "innerwordly" kinds of behaviour: those, in other words, concerning man's relationship with himself, with others and with the material world. There thus appears to be established within human acting a clear disjunction between two levels of morality: on the one hand the order of good and evil, which is dependent on the will, and on the other hand specific kinds of behaviour, which are judged to be morally right or wrong only on the basis of a technical calculation of the proportion between the "premoral" or "physical" goods and evils which actually result from the action. This is pushed to the point where a concrete kind of behaviour, even one freely chosen, comes to be considered as a merely physical process, and not according to the criteria proper to a human act. The conclusion to which this eventually leads is that the properly moral assessment of the person is reserved to his fundamental option, prescinding in whole or in part from his choice of particular actions, of concrete kinds of behaviour.

66. There is no doubt that Christian moral teaching, even in its biblical roots, acknowledges the specific importance of a fundamental choice which qualifies the moral life and engages freedom on a radical level before God. It is a question of the decision of faith, of the *obedience of faith* (cf. *Rom* 16:26) "by which man makes a total and free self-commitment to God, offering 'the full submission of intellect and will to God as he reveals'".[112] This faith, which works through love (cf. *Gal* 5:6), comes from the core of man, from his "heart" (cf. *Rom* 10:10), whence it is called to bear fruit in works (cf. *Mt* 12:33–35; *Lk* 6:43–45; *Rom* 8:5–10; *Gal* 5:22). In the Decalogue one finds, as an introduction to the various commandments, the basic clause: "I am the Lord your God ..." (*Ex* 20:2), which, by impressing upon the numerous and varied particular prescriptions their primordial meaning, gives the morality of the Covenant its aspect of completeness, unity and profundity. Israel's fundamental decision, then, is about the fundamental commandment (cf. *Jos* 24:14–25; *Ex* 19:3–8; *Mic* 6:8). The morality of the New Covenant is similarly dominated by the fundamental call of Jesus to follow him—thus he also says to the young man: "If you wish to be perfect ... then come, follow me" (*Mt* 19:21); to this call the disciple must respond with a radical decision and choice. The Gospel parables of the treasure and the pearl of great price, for which one sells all one's possessions, are eloquent and effective images of the radical and unconditional nature of the decision demanded by the Kingdom of God. The radical nature of the decision to follow Jesus is admirably expressed in his own words: "Whoever would save his life will lose it; and whoever loses his life for my sake and the Gospel's will save it" (*Mk* 8:35).

Jesus' call to "come, follow me" marks the greatest possible exaltation of human freedom, yet at the same time it witnesses to the truth and to the obligation of acts of faith and of decisions which can be described as involving a fundamental option. We find a similar exaltation of human freedom in the words of Saint Paul: "You were called to freedom, brethren" (*Gal* 5:13). But the Apostle immediately adds a grave warning: "Only do not use your freedom as an opportunity for the flesh". This warning echoes his earlier words: "For freedom Christ has set us free; stand fast therefore, and do not submit again to a yoke of slavery" (*Gal*

---

[112] SECOND VATICAN ECUMENICAL COUNCIL, Dogmatic Constitution on Divine Revelation, *Dei Verbum*, 5; cf. FIRST VATICAN ECUMENICAL COUNCIL, Dogmatic Constitution on the Catholic Faith *Dei Filius*, Chap. 3: *DS*, 3008.

5:1). Paul encourages us to be watchful, because freedom is always threatened by slavery. And this is precisely the case when an act of faith—in the sense of a fundamental option—becomes separated from the choice of particular acts, as in the tendencies mentioned above.

67. These tendencies are therefore contrary to the teaching of Scripture itself, which sees the fundamental option as a genuine choice of freedom and links that choice profoundly to particular acts. By his fundamental choice, man is capable of giving his life direction and of progressing, with the help of grace, towards his end, following God's call. But this capacity is actually exercised in the particular choices of specific actions, through which man deliberately conforms himself to God's will, wisdom and law. It thus needs to be stated that *the so-called fundamental option, to the extent that it is distinct from a generic intention and hence one not yet determined in such a way that freedom is obligated, is always brought into play through conscious and free decisions.* Precisely for this reason, *it is revoked when man engages his freedom in conscious decisions to the contrary, with regard to morally grave matter.*

To separate the fundamental option from concrete kinds of behaviour means to contradict the substantial integrity or personal unity of the moral agent in his body and in his soul. A fundamental option understood without explicit consideration of the potentialities which it puts into effect and the determinations which express it does not do justice to the rational finality immanent in man's acting and in each of his deliberate decisions. In point of fact, the morality of human acts is not deduced only from one's intention, orientation or fundamental option, understood as an intention devoid of a clearly determined binding content or as an intention with no corresponding positive effort to fulfil the different obligations of the moral life. Judgments about morality cannot be made without taking into consideration whether or not the deliberate choice of a specific kind of behaviour is in conformity with the dignity and integral vocation of the human person. Every choice always implies a reference by the deliberate will to the goods and evils indicated by the natural law as goods to be pursued and evils to be avoided. In the case of the positive moral precepts, prudence always has the task of verifying that they apply in a specific situation, for example, in view of other duties which may be more important or urgent. But the negative moral precepts, those prohibiting certain concrete actions or kinds of behaviour as intrinsically evil, do not allow for any legitimate exception. They do not leave room, in any morally acceptable way, for the "creativity" of any contrary determination whatsoever. Once the moral species of an action prohibited by a universal rule is concretely recognized, the only morally good act is that of obeying the moral law and of refraining from the action which it forbids.

68. Here an important pastoral consideration must be added. According to the logic of the positions mentioned above, an individual could, by virtue of a fundamental option, remain faithful to God independently of whether or not certain of his choices and his acts are in conformity with specific moral norms or rules. By virtue of a primordial option for charity, that individual could continue to be morally good, persevere in God's grace and attain salvation, even if certain of his specific kinds of behaviour were deliberately and gravely contrary to God's commandments as set forth by the Church.

In point of fact, man does not suffer perdition only by being unfaithful to that fundamental option whereby he has made "a free self-commitment to God".[113] With every freely committed mortal sin, he offends God as the giver of the law and as a result becomes guilty with regard to the entire law (cf. *Jas* 2:8–11); even if he perseveres in faith, he loses "sanctifying grace", "charity" and "eternal happiness".[114] As the Council of Trent teaches, "the grace of justification once received is lost not only by apostasy, by which faith itself is lost, but also by any other mortal sin".[115]

Mortal and venial sin

69. As we have just seen, reflection on the fundamental option has also led some theologians to undertake a basic revision of the traditional distinction between *mortal* sins and *venial* sins. They insist that the opposition to God's law which causes the loss of sanctifying grace—and eternal damnation, when one dies in such a state of sin—could only be the result of an act which engages the person in his totality: in other words, an act of fundamental option. According to these theologians, mortal sin, which separates man from God, only exists in the rejection of God, carried out at a level of freedom which is neither to be identified with an act of choice nor capable of becoming the object of conscious awareness. Consequently, they go on to say, it is difficult, at least psychologically, to accept the fact that a Christian, who wishes to remain united to Jesus Christ and to his Church, could so easily and repeatedly

---

[113] SECOND VATICAN ECUMENICAL COUNCIL, Dogmatic Constitution of Divine Revelation *Dei Verbum*, 5. Cf. SACRED CONGREGATION FOR THE DOCTRINE OF THE FAITH, Declaration on certain Questions regarding Sexual Ethics *Persona Humana* (29 December 1975), 10: *AAS* 68 (1976), 88–90.

[114] Cf. Post-Synodal Apostolic Exhortation *Reconciliatio et Paenitentia* (2 December 1984), 17: *AAS* 77 (1985), 218–223.

[115] Sess. VI, Decree on Justification *Cum Hoc Tempore*, Chap. 15: *DS*, 1544; Canon 19: *DS*, 1569.

commit mortal sins, as the "matter" itself of his actions would sometimes indicate. Likewise, it would be hard to accept that man is able, in a brief lapse of time, to sever radically the bond of communion with God and afterwards be converted to him by sincere repentance. The gravity of sin, they maintain, ought to be measured by the degree of engagement of the freedom of the person performing an act, rather than by the matter of that act.

70.   The Post-Synodal Apostolic Exhortation *Reconciliatio et Paenitentia* reaffirmed the importance and permanent validity of the distinction between mortal and venial sins, in accordance with the Church's tradition. And the 1983 Synod of Bishops, from which that Exhortation emerged, "not only reaffirmed the teaching of the Council of Trent concerning the existence and nature of mortal and venial sins, but is also recalled that mortal sin is sin whose object is grave matter and which is also committed with full knowledge and deliberate consent".[116]

The statement of the Council of Trent does not only consider the "grave matter" of mortal sin; it also recalls that its necessary condition is "full awareness and deliberate consent". In any event, both in moral theology and in pastoral practice one is familiar with cases in which an act which is grave by reason of its matter does not constitute a mortal sin because of a lack of full awareness or deliberate consent on the part of the person performing it. Even so, "care will have to be taken not to reduce mortal sin to an act of *'fundamental option'*—as is commonly said today— against God", seen either as an explicit and formal rejection of God and neighbour or as an implicit and unconscious rejection of love. "For mortal sin exists also when a person knowingly and willingly, for whatever reason, chooses something gravely disordered. In fact, such a choice already includes contempt for the divine law, a rejection of God's love for humanity and the whole of creation: the person turns away from God and loses charity. Consequently, *the fundamental orientation can be radically changed by particular acts.* Clearly, situations can occur which are very complex and obscure from a psychological viewpoint, and which influence the sinner's subjective imputability. But from a considera- tion of the psychological sphere one cannot proceed to create a theological category, which is pecisely what the 'fundamental option' is, understand- ing it in such a way that it objectively changes or casts doubt upon the traditional concept of mortal sin".[117]

The separation of fundamental option from deliberate choices of

---

[116] Post-Synodal Apostolic Exhortation *Reconciliatio et Paenitentia* (2 December 1984), 17: *AAS* 77 (1985), 221.
[117] *Ibid.: loc. cit.,* 223.

particular kinds of behaviour, disordered in themselves or in their circumstances, which would not engage that option, thus involves a denial of Catholic doctrine on *mortal sin*: "With the whole tradition of the Church, we call mortal sin the act by which man freely and consciously rejects God, his law, the covenant of love that God offers, preferring to turn in on himself or to some created and finite reality, something contrary to the divine will (*conversio ad creaturam*). This can occur in a direct and formal way, in the sins of idolatry, apostasy and atheism; or in an equivalent way, as in every act of disobedience to God's commandments in a grave matter".[118]

IV. THE MORAL ACT

Teleology and teleologism

71.   The relationship between man's freedom and God's law, which has its intimate and living centre in the moral conscience, is manifested and realized in human acts. It is precisely through his acts that man attains perfection as man, as one who is called to seek his Creator of his own accord and freely to arrive at full and blessed perfection by cleaving to him.[119]

Human acts are moral acts because they express and determine the goodness or evil of the individual who performs them.[120] They do not produce a change merely in the state of affairs outside of man but, to the extent that they are deliberate choices, they give moral definition to the very person who performs them, determining his *profound spiritual traits*. This was perceptively noted by Saint Gregory of Nyssa: "All things subject to change and to becoming never remain constant, but continually pass from one state to another, for better or worse ... Now, human life is always subject to change; it needs to be born ever anew ... But here birth does not come about by a foreign intervention, as is the case with bodily beings ...; it is the result of a free choice. Thus *we are* in a certain way our own parents, creating ourselves as we will, by our decisions".[121]

---

[118] *Ibid.: loc. cit.,* 222.

[119] Cf. SECOND VATICAN ECUMENICAL COUNCIL, Pastoral Constitution on the Church in the Modern World *Gaudium et Spes,* 17.

[120] Cf. SAINT THOMAS AQUINAS, *Summa Theologiae,* I–II, q. 1, a. 3: "Idem sunt actus morales et actus humani".

[121] *De Vita Moysis,* II, 2–3: PG 44, 327–328.

72. The *morality of acts* is defined by the relationship of man's freedom with the authentic good. This good is established, as the eternal law, by Divine Wisdom which orders every being towards its end: this eternal law is known both by man's natural reason (hence it is "natural law"), and—in an integral and perfect way—by God's supernatural Revelation (hence it is called "divine law"). Acting is morally good when the choices of freedom are *in conformity with man's true good* and thus express the voluntary ordering of the person towards his ultimate end: God himself, the supreme good in whom man finds his full and perfect happiness. The first question in the young man's conversation with Jesus: "What good must I do to have eternal life?" (*Mt* 19:6) immediately brings out *the essential connection between the moral value of an act and man's final end.* Jesus, in his reply, confirms the young man's conviction: the performance of good acts, commanded by the One who "alone is good", constitutes the indispensable condition of and path to eternal blessedness: "If you wish to enter into life, keep the commandments" (*Mt* 19:17). Jesus' answer and his reference to the commandments also make it clear that the path to that end is marked by respect for the divine laws which safeguard human good. *Only the act in conformity with the good can be a path that leads to life.*

The rational ordering of the human act to the good in its truth and the voluntary pursuit of that good, known by reason, constitute morality. Hence human activity cannot be judged as morally good merely because it is a means for attaining one or another of its goals, or simply because the subject's intention is good.[122] Activity is morally good when it attests to and expresses the voluntary ordering of the person to his ultimate end and the conformity of a concrete action with the human good as it is acknowledged in its truth by reason. If the object of the concrete action is not in harmony with the true good of the person, the choice of that action makes our will and ourselves morally evil, thus putting us in conflict with our ultimate end, the supreme good, God himself.

73. The Christian, thanks to God's Revelation and to faith, is aware of the "newness" which characterizes the morality of his actions: these actions are called to show either consistency or inconsistency with that dignity and vocation which have been bestowed on him by grace. In Jesus Christ and in his Spirit, the Christian is a "new creation", a child of God; by his actions he shows his likeness or unlikeness to the image of the Son who is the first-born among many brethren (cf. *Rom* 8:29), he lives out his fidelity or infidelity to the gift of the Spirit, and he opens or

---

[122] Cf. SAINT THOMAS AQUINAS, *Summa Theologiae*, II–II, q. 148, a. 3.

closes himself to eternal life, to the communion of vision, love and happiness with God the Father, Son and Holy Spirit.[123] As Saint Cyril of Alexandria writes, Christ "forms us according to his image, in such a way that the traits of his divine nature shine forth in us through sanctification and justice and the life which is good and in conformity with virtue ... The beauty of this image shines forth in us who are in Christ, when we show ourselves to be good in our works".[124]

Consequently the moral life has an essential *"teleological" character*, since it consists in the deliberate ordering of human acts to God, the supreme good and ultimate end (*telos*) of man. This is attested to once more by the question posed by the young man to Jesus: "What good must I do to have eternal life?" But this ordering to one's ultimate end is not something subjective, dependent solely upon one's intention. It presupposes that such acts are in themselves capable of being ordered to this end, insofar as they are in conformity with the authentic moral good of man, safeguarded by the commandments. This is what Jesus himself points out in his reply to the young man: "If you wish to enter into life, keep the commandments" (*Mt* 19:17).

Clearly such an ordering must be rational and free, conscious and deliberate, by virtue of which man is "responsible" for his actions and subject to the judgment of God, the just and good judge who, as the Apostle Paul reminds us, rewards good and punishes evil: "We must all appear before the judgment seat of Christ, so that each one may receive good or evil, according to what he has done in the body" (*2 Cor* 5:10).

74. But on what does the moral assessment of man's free acts depend? What is it that ensures this *ordering of human acts to God?* Is it the *intention* of the acting subject, the *circumstances*—and in particular the consequences—of his action, or the *object* itself of his act?

This is what is traditionally called the problem of the "sources of morality". Precisely with regard to this problem there have emerged in the last few decades new or newly-revived theological and cultural trends which call for careful discernment on the part of the Church's Magisterium.

---

[123] The Second Vatican Council, in the Pastoral Constitution on the Church in the Modern World, makes this clear: "This applies not only to Christians but to all men of good will in whose hearts grace is secretly at work. Since Christ died for all and since man's ultimate calling comes from God and is therefore a universal one, we are obliged to hold that the Holy Spirit offers to all the possibility of sharing in this paschal mystery in a manner known to God": *Gaudium et Spes*, 22.

[124] *Tractatus ad Tiberium Diaconum sociosque, II. Responsiones ad Tiberium Diaconum sociosque:* SAINT CYRIL OF ALEXANDRIA, *In Divi Johannis Evangelium*, vol. III, ed. Philip Edward Pusey, Brussels, Culture et Civilisation (1965), 590.

Certain *ethical theories*, called *"telelogical"*, claim to be concerned for the conformity of human acts with the ends pursued by the agent and with the values intended by him. The criteria for evaluating the moral rightness of an action are drawn from the *weighing of the non-moral or pre-moral goods* to be gained and the corresponding non-moral or pre-moral values to be respected. For some, concrete behaviour would be right or wrong according as whether or not it is capable of producing a better state of affairs for all concerned. Right conduct would be the one capable of "maximizing" goods and "minimizing" evils.

Many of the Catholic moralists who follow in this direction seek to distance themselves from utilitarianism and pragmatism, where the morality of human acts would be judged without any reference to the man's true ultimate end. They rightly recognize the need to find ever more consistent rational arguments in order to justify the requirements and to provide a foundation for the norms of the moral life. This kind of invetigation is legitimate and necessary, since the moral order, as established by the natural law, is in principle accessible to human reason. Furthermore, such investigation is well-suited to meeting the demands of dialogue and cooperation with non-Catholics and non-believers, especially in pluralistic societies.

75.   But as part of the effort to work out such a rational morality (for this reason it is sometimes called an "autonomous morality") there exist *false solutions, linked in particular to an inadequate understanding of the object of moral action. Some authors* do not take into sufficient consideration the fact that the will is involved in the concrete choices which it makes: these choices are a condition of its moral goodness and its being ordered to the ultimate end of the person. *Others* are inspired by a notion of freedom which prescinds from the actual conditions of its exercise, from its objective reference to the truth about the good, and from its determination through choices of concrete kinds of behaviour. According to these theories, free will would neither be morally subjected to specific obligations nor shaped by its choices, while nonetheless still remaining responsible for its own acts and for their consequences. This *"teleologism"*, as a method for discovering the moral norm, can thus be called—according to terminology and approaches imported from different currents of thought—*"consequentialism"* or *"proportionalism'*. The former claims to draw the criteria of the rightness of a given way of acting solely from a calculation of foreseeable consequences deriving from a given choice. The latter, by weighing the various values and goods being sought, focuses rather on the proportion acknowledged between the good and bad effects of that choice, with a view to the "greater good" or "lesser evil" actually possible in a particular situation.

The teleological ethical theories (proportionalism, consequentialism), while acknowledging that moral values are indicated by reason and by Revelation, maintain that it is never possible to formulate an absolute prohibition of particular kinds of behaviour which would be in conflict, in every circumstance and in every culture, with those values. The acting subject would indeed be responsible for attaining the values pursued, but in two ways: the values or goods involved in a human act would be, from one viewpoint, *of the moral order* (in relation to properly moral values, such as love of God and neighbour, justice, etc.) and, from another viewpoint, *of the pre-moral order*, which some term non-moral, physical or ontic (in relation to the advantages and disadvantages accruing both to the agent and to all other persons possibly involved, such as, for example, health or its endangerment, physical integrity, life, death, loss of material goods, etc.). In a world where goodness is always mixed with evil, and every good effect linked to other evil effects, the morality of an act would be judged in two different ways: its moral "goodness" would be judged on the basis of the subject's intention in reference to moral goods, and its "rightness" on the basis of a consideration of its foreseeable effects or consequences and of their proportion. Consequently, concrete kinds of behaviour could be described as "right" or "wrong", without it being thereby possible to judge as morally "good" or "bad" the will of the person choosing them. In this way, an act which, by contradicting a universal negative norm, directly violates goods considered as "pre-moral" could be qualified as morally acceptable if the intention of the subject is focused, in accordance with a "responsible" assessment of the goods involved in the concrete action, on the moral value judged to be decisive in the situation.

The evaluation of the consequences of the action, based on the proportion between the act and its effects and between the effects themselves, would regard only the pre-moral order. The moral specificity of acts, that is their goodness or evil, would be determined exclusively by the faithfulness of the person to the highest values of charity and prudence, without this faithfulness necessarily being incompatible with choices contrary to certain particular moral precepts. Even when grave matter is concerned, these precepts should be considered as operative norms which are always relative and open to exceptions.

In this view, deliberate consent to certain kinds of behaviour declared illicit by traditional moral theology would not imply an objective moral evil.

The object of the deliberate act

76.   These theories can gain a certain persuasive force from their

affinity to the scientific mentality, which is rightly concerned with ordering technical and economic activities on the basis of a calculation of resources and profits, procedures and their effects. They seek to provide liberation from the constraints of a voluntaristic and arbitrary morality of obligation which would ultimately be dehumanizing.

Such theories however are not faithful to the Church's teaching, when they believe they can justify, as morally good, deliberate choices of kinds of behaviour contrary to the commandments of the divine and natural law. These theories cannot claim to be grounded in the Catholic moral tradition. Although the latter did witness the development of a casuistry which tried to assess the best ways to achieve the good in certain concrete situations, it is nonetheless true that this casuistry concerned only cases in which the law was uncertain, and thus the absolute validity of negative moral precepts, which oblige without exception, was not called into question. The faithful are obliged to acknowledge and respect the specific moral precepts declared and taught by the Church in the name of God, the Creator and Lord.[125] When the Apostle Paul sums up the fulfilment of the law in the precept of love of neighbour as oneself (cf. *Rom* 13:8-10), he is not weakening the commandments but reinforcing them, since he is revealing their requirements and their gravity. *Love of God and of one's neighbour cannot be separated from the observance of the commandments of the Covenant* renewed in the blood of Jesus Christ and in the gift of the Spirit. It is an honour characteristic of Christians to obey God rather than men (cf. *Acts* 4:19; 5:29) and accept even martyrdom as a consequence, like the holy men and women of the Old and New Testaments, who are considered such because they gave thier lives rather than perform this or that particular act contrary to faith or virtue.

77.   In order to offer rational criteria for a right moral decision, the theories mentioned above take account of the intention and *consequences* of human action. Certainly there is need to take into account both the intention—as Jesus forcefully insisted in clear disagreement with the scribes and Pharisees, who prescribed in great detail certain outward practices without paying attention to the heart (cf. *Mk* 7:20-21; *Mt* 15:19)—and the goods obtained and the evils avoided as a result of a particular act. Responsibility demands as much. But the consideration of these consequences, and also of intentions, is not sufficient for judging the moral quality of a concrete choice. The weighing of the goods and

---

[125] Cf. ECUMENICAL COUNCIL OF TRENT, Session VI, Decree on Justification *Cum Hoc Tempore*, Canon 19: *DS*, 1569. See also: CLEMENT XI, Constitution *Unigenitus Dei Filius* [8 September 1713] against the Errors of Paschasius Quesnel, Nos. 53–56: *DS*, 2453–2456.

evils foreseeable as the consequence of an action is not an adequate method for determining whether the choice of that concrete kind of behaviour is "according to its species", or "in itself", morally good or bad, licit or illicit. The foreseeable consequences are part of those circumstances of the act, which, while capable of lessening the gravity of an evil act, nonetheless cannot alter its moral species.

Moreover, everyone recognizes the difficulty, or rather the impossibility, of evaluating all the good and evil consequences and effects—defined as pre-moral—of one's own acts: an exhaustive rational calculation is not possible. How then can one go about establishing proportions which depend on a measuring, the criteria of which remain obscure? How could an absolute obligation be justified on the basis of such debatable calculations?

78.   *The morality of the human act depends primarily and fundamentally on the "object" rationally chosen by the deliberate will,* as is borne out by the insightful analysis, still valid today, made by Saint Thomas.[126] In order to be able to grasp the object of an act which specifies that act morally, it is therefore necessary to place oneself *in the perspective of the acting person.* The object of the act of willing is in fact a freely chosen kind of behaviour. To the extent that it is in conformity with the order of reason, it is the cause of the goodness of the will; it perfects us morally, and disposes us to recognize our ultimate end in the perfect good, primordial love. By the object of a given moral act, then, one cannot mean a process or an event of the merely physical order, to be assessed on the basis of its ability to bring about a given state of affairs in the outside world. Rather, that object is the proximate end of a deliberate decision which determines the act of willing on the part of the acting person. Consequently, as the *Catechism of the Catholic Church* teaches, "there are certain specific kinds of behaviour that are always wrong to choose, because choosing them involves a disorder of the will, that is, a moral evil".[127] And Saint Thomas observes that "it often happens that man acts with a good intention, but without spiritual gain, because he lacks a good will. Let us say that someone robs in order to feed the poor: in this case, even though the intention is good, the uprightness of the will is lacking. Consequently, no evil done with a good intention can be excused. 'There are those who say: And why not do evil that good may come? Their condemnation is just' (*Rom* 3:8)".[128]

---

[126] Cf. *Summa Theologiae*, I–II, q. 18, a. 6.

[127] *Catechism of the Catholic Church*, No. 1761.

[128] *In Duo Praecepta Caritatis et in Decem Legis Praecepta. De Dilectione Dei: Opuscula Theologica,* II, No. 1168, Ed. Taurinen (1954), 250.

The reason why a good intention is not itself sufficient, but a correct choice of actions is also needed, is that the human act depends on its object, whether that object is *capable or not of being ordered* to God, to the One who "alone is good", and thus brings about the perfection of the person. An act is therefore good if its object is in conformity with the good of the person with respect for the goods morally relevant for him. Christian ethics, which pays particular attention to the moral object, does not refuse to consider the inner "teleology" of acting, inasmuch as it is directed to promoting the true good of the person; but it recognizes that it is really pursued only when the essential elements of human nature are respected. The human act, good according to its object, is also *capable of being ordered* to its ultimate end. That same act then attains its ultimate and decisive perfection when the will *actually does order* it to God through charity. As the Patron of moral theologians and confessors teaches: "It is not enough to do good works; they need to be done well. For our works to be good and perfect, they must be done for the sole purpose of pleasing God".[129]

"Intrinsic evil": it is not licit to do evil that good may come of it (cf. *Rom* 3:8)

79.   *One must therefore reject the thesis,* characteristic of teleological and proportionalist theories, *which holds that it is impossible to qualify as morally evil according to its species—its "object"—the deliberate choice of certain kinds of behaviour or specific acts, apart from a consideration of the intention for which the choice is made or the totality of the foreseeable consequences of that act for all persons concerned.*

The primary and decisive element for moral judgment is the object of the human act, which establishes whether it is *capable of being ordered to the good and to the ultimate end, which is God.* This capability is grasped by reason in the very being of man, considered in his integral truth, and therefore in his natural inclinations, his motivations and his finalities, which always have a spiritual dimension as well. It is precisely these which are the contents of the natural law and hence that ordered complex of "personal goods" which serve the "good of the person": the good which is the person himself and his perfection. These are the goods safeguarded by the commandments, which, according to Saint Thomas, contain the whole natural law.[130]

---

[129] SAINT ALPHONSUS MARIA DE' LIGUORI, *Pratica di amar Gesù Cristo,* VII, 3.
[130] Cf. *Summa Theologiae,* I-II, q. 100, a. 1.

149

80. Reason attests that there are objects of the human act which are by their nature "incapable of being ordered" to God, because they radically contradict the good of the person made in his image. These are the acts which, in the Church's moral tradition, have been termed "intrinsically evil" (*intrinsece malum*): they are such *always and per se*, in other words, on account of their very object, and quite apart from the ulterior intentions of the one acting and the circumstances. Consequently, without in the least denying the influence on morality exercised by circumstances and especially by intentions, the Church teaches that "there exist acts which *per se* and in themselves, independently of circumstances, are always seriously wrong by reason of their object".[131] The Second Vatican Council itself, in discussing the respect due to the human person, gives a number of examples of such acts: "Whatever is hostile to life itself, such as any kind of homicide, genocide, abortion, euthanasia and voluntary suicide; whatever violates the integrity of the human person, such as mutilation, physical and mental torture and attempts to coerce the spirit; whatever is offensive to human dignity, such as subhuman living conditions, arbitrary imprisonment, deportation, slavery, prostitution and trafficking in women and children; degrading conditions of work which treat labourers as mere instruments of profit, and not as free responsible persons: all these and the like are a disgrace, and so long as they infect human civilization they contaminate those who inflict them more than those who suffer injustice, and they are a negation of the honour due to the Creator".[132]

With regard to intrinsically evil acts, and in reference to contraceptive practices whereby the conjugal act is intentionally rendered infertile, Pope Paul VI teaches: "Though it is true that sometimes it is lawful to tolerate a lesser moral evil in order to avoid a greater evil or in order to promote a greater good, it is never lawful, even for the gravest reasons, to do evil that good may come of it (cf. *Rom* 3:8)—in other words, to intend directly something which of its very nature contradicts the moral order, and which must therefore be judged unworthy of man, even though the intention is to protect or promote the welfare of an individual, of a family or of society in general".[133]

---

[131] Post-Synodal Apostolic Exhortation *Reconciliatio et Paenitentia* (2 December 1984), 17: *AAS* 77 (1985), 221; cf. PAUL VI, *Address* to Members of the Congregation of the Most Holy Redeemer (September 1967): *AAS* 59 (1967), 962: "Far be it from Christians to be led to embrace another opinion, as if the Council taught that nowadays some things are permitted which the Church had previously declared intrinsically evil. Who does not see in this the rise of a depraved *moral relativism*, one that clearly endangers the Church's entire doctrinal heritage?"

[132] Pastoral Constitution on the Church in the Modern World *Gaudium et Spes*, 27.

[133] Encyclical Letter *Humanae Vitae* (25 July 1968), 14: *AAS* 60 (1968), 490–491.

81. In teaching the existence of intrinsically evil acts, the Church accepts the teaching of Sacred Scripture. The Apostle Paul emphatically states: "Do not be deceived: neither the immoral, nor idolaters, nor adulterers, nor sexual perverts, nor thieves, nor the greedy, nor drunkards, nor revilers, nor robbers will inherit the Kingdom of God" (1 Cor 6:9–10).

If acts are intrinsically evil, a good intention or particular circumstances can diminish their evil, but they cannot remove it. They remain "irremediably" evil acts; per se and in themselves they are not capable of being ordered to God and to the good of the person. "As for acts which are themselves sins (cum iam opera ipsa peccata sunt), Saint Augustine writes, like theft, fornication, blasphemy, who would dare affirm that, by doing them for good motives (causis bonis), they would no longer be sins, or, what is even more absurd, that they would be sins that are justified?"[134]

Consequently, circumstances or intentions can never transform an act intrinsically evil by virtue of its object into an act "subjectively" good or defensible as a choice.

82. Furthermore, an intention is good when it has as its aim the true good of the person in view of his ultimate end. But acts whose object is "not capable of being ordered" to God and "unworthy of the human person" are always and in every case in conflict with that good. Consequently, respect for norms which prohibit such acts and oblige semper et pro semper, that is, without any exception, not only does not inhibit a good intention, but actually represents its basic expression.

The doctrine of the object as a source of morality represents an authentic explicitation of the Biblical morality of the Covenant and of the commandments, of charity and of the virtues. The moral quality of human acting is dependent on this fidelity to the commandments, as an expression of obedience and of love. For this reason—we repeat—the opinion must be rejected as erroneous which maintains that it is impossible to qualify as morally evil according to its species the deliberate choice of certain kinds of behaviour or specific acts, without taking into account the intention for which the choice was made or the totality of the foreseeable consequences of that act for all persons concerned. Without the rational determination of the morality of human acting as stated above, it would be impossible to affirm the existence of an "objective moral order"[135] and to establish any particular norm the content of which

---

[134] Contra Mendacium, VII, 18: PL 40, 528; cf. SAINT THOMAS AQUINAS, Quaestiones Quodlibetales, IX, q. 7, a. 2; Catechism of the Catholic Church, Nos. 1753–1755.

[135] SECOND VATICAN ECUMENICAL COUNCIL, Declaration on Religious Freedom Dignitatis Humanae, 7.

would be binding without exception. This would be to the detriment of human fraternity and the truth about the good, and would be injurious to ecclesial communion as well.

83. As is evident, in the question of the morality of human acts, and in particular the question of whether there exist intrinsically evil acts, we find ourselves faced with *the question of man himself,* of his *truth* and of the moral consequences flowing from that truth. By acknowledging and teaching the existence of intrinsic evil in given human acts, the Church remains faithful to the integral truth about man; she thus respects and promotes man in his dignity and vocation. Consequently, she must reject the theories set forth above, which contradict this truth.

Dear Brothers in the Episcopate, we must not be content merely to warn the faithful about the errors and dangers of certain ethical theories. We must first of all show the inviting splendour of that truth which is Jesus Christ himself. In him, who is the Truth (cf. *Jn* 14:6), man can understand fully and live perfectly, through his good actions, his vocation to freedom in obedience to the divine law summarized in the commandment of love of God and neighbour. And this is what takes place through the gift of the Holy Spirit, the Spirit of truth, of freedom and of love: in him we are enabled to interiorize the law, to receive it and to live it as the motivating force of true personal freedom: "the perfect law, the law of liberty" (*Jas* 1:25).

CHAPTER THREE

"LEST THE CROSS OF CHRIST BE EMPTIED OF ITS POWER"

(1 Cor 1:17)

MORAL GOOD FOR THE LIFE OF THE CHURCH AND OF THE WORLD

"For freedom Christ has set us free" (Gal 5:1)

84.   The *fundamental question* which the moral theories mentioned above pose in a particularly forceful way is that of the relationship of man's freedom to God's law; it is ultimately the question of the *relationship between freedom and truth.*

According to Christian faith and the Church's teaching, "only the freedom which submits to the Truth leads the human person to his true good. The good of the person is to be in the Truth and to *do* the Truth".[136]

A comparison between the Church's teaching and today's social and cultural situation immediately makes clear the urgent need *for the church herself to develop an intense pastoral effort precisely with regard to this fundamental question.* "This essential bond between Truth, the Good and Freedom has been largely lost sight of by present-day culture. As a result,

---

[136] *Address* to those taking part in the International Congress of Moral Theology (10 April 1986), 1: *Insegnamenti* IX, 1 (1986), 970.

helping man to rediscover it represents nowadays one of the specific requirements of the Church's mission, for the salvation of the world. Pilate's question: 'What is truth' reflects the distressing perplexity of a man who often no longer knows *who he is, whence* he comes and *where* he is going. Hence we not infrequently witness the fearful plunging of the human person into situations of gradual self-destruction. According to some, it appears that one no longer need acknowledge the enduring absoluteness of any moral value. All around us we encounter contempt for human life after conception and before birth; the ongoing violation of basic rights of the person; the unjust destruction of goods minimally necessary for a human life. Indeed, something more serious has happened: man is no longer convinced that only in the truth can he find salvation. The saving power of truth is contested, and freedom alone, uprooted from any objectivity, is left to decide by itself what is good and what is evil. This relativism becomes, in the field of theology, a lack of trust in the wisdom of God, who guides man with the moral law. Concrete situations are unfavourably contrasted with the precepts of the moral law, nor is it any longer maintained that, when all is said and done, the law of God is always the one true good of man".[137]

85   The discernment which the Church carries out with regard to these ethical theories is not simply limited to denouncing and refuting them. In a positive way, the Church seeks, with great love, to help all the faithful to form a moral conscience which will make judgments and lead to decisions in accordance with the truth, following the exhortation of the Apostle Paul: "Do not be conformed to this world but be transformed by the renewal of your mind, that you may prove what is the will of God, what is good and acceptable and perfect" (*Rom* 12:2). This effort by the Church finds it support—the "secret" of its educative power—not so much in doctrinal statements and pastoral appeals to vigilance, as in *constantly looking to the Lord Jesus.* Each day the Church looks to Christ with unfailing love, fully aware that the true and final answer to the problem of morality lies in him alone. In a particular way, it is *in the Crucified Christ* that *the Church finds the answer* to the question troubling so many people today: how can obedience to universal and unchanging moral norms respect the uniqueness and individuality of the person, and not represent a threat to his freedom and dignity? The Church makes her own the Apostle Paul's awareness of the mission he had received: "Christ ... sent me ... to preach the Gospel, and not with eloquent wisdom, lest the cross of Christ be emptied of its power ... We preach Christ

[137] *Ibid.,* 2: *loc. cit.,* 970–971.

crucified, a stumbling block to Jews and folly to Gentiles, but to those who are called, both Jews and Greeks, Christ the power of God and the wisdom of God" (*1 Cor* 1:17, 23–24). *The Crucified Christ reveals the authentic meaning of freedom; he lives it fully in the total gift of himself* and calls his disciples to share in his freedom.

86. Rational reflection and daily experience demonstrate the weakness which marks man's freedom. That freedom is real but limited: its absolute and unconditional origin is not in itself, but in the life within which it is situated and which represents for it, at one and the same time, both a limitation and a possibility. Human freedom belongs to us as creatures; it is a freedom which is given as a gift, one to be received like a seed and to be cultivated responsibly. It is an essential part of that creaturely image which is the basis of the dignity of the person. Within that freedom there is an echo of the primordial vocation whereby the Creator calls man to the true Good, and even more, through Christ's Revelation, to become his friend and to share his own divine life. It is at once inalienable self-possession and openness to all that exists, in passing beyond self to knowledge and love of the other.[138] Freedom then is rooted in the truth about man, and it is ultimately directed towards communion.

Reason and experience not only confirm the weakness of human freedom; they also confirm its tragic aspects. Man comes to realize that his freedom is in some mysterious way inclined to betray this openness to the True and the Good, and that all too often he actually prefers to choose finite, limited and ephemeral goods. What is more, within his errors and negative decisions, man glimpses the source of a deep rebellion, which leads him to reject the Truth and the Good in order to set himself up as an absolute principle unto himself: "You will be like God" (*Gen* 3:5). Consequently, *freedom itself needs to be set free. It is Christ who sets it free*: he "has set us free for freedom" (cf. *Gal* 5:1).

87. Christ reveals, first and foremost, that the frank and open acceptance of truth is the condition for authentic freedom: "You will know the truth, and the truth will set you free" (*Jn* 8:32).[139] This is truth which sets one free in the face of wordly power and which gives the strength to endure martyrdom. So it was with Jesus before Pilate: "For this I was born, and for this I have come into the world, to bear witness

[138] Cf. SECOND VATICAN ECUMENICAL COUNCIL, Pastoral Constitution on the Church in the Modern World *Gaudium et Spes*, 24.

[139] Cf. Encyclical Letter *Redemptor Hominis* (4 March 1979), 12: *AAS* 71 (1979), 280–281.

to the truth" (*Jn* 18:37). The true worshippers of God must thus worship him "in spirit and truth" (*Jn* 4:23): *in this worship they become free*. Worship of God and a relationship with truth are revealed in Jesus Christ as the deepest foundation of freedom.

Furthermore, Jesus reveals by his whole life, and not only by his words, that freedom is acquired in *love*, that is, in the *gift of self*. The one who says: "Greater love has no man than this, that a man lay down his life for his friends" (*Jn* 15:13), freely goes out to meet his Passion (cf. *Mt* 26:46), and in obedience to the Father gives his life on the Cross for all men (cf. *Phil* 2:6–11). Contemplation of Jesus Crucified is thus the highroad which the Church must tread every day if she wishes to understand the full meaning of freedom: the gift of self in *service to God and one's brethren*. Communion with the Crucified and Risen Lord is the never-ending source from which the Church draws unceasingly in order to live in freedom, to give of herself and to serve. Commenting on the verse in Psalm 100 "Serve the Lord with gladness", Saint Augustine says: "In the house of the Lord, slavery is free. It is free because it serves not out of necessity, but out of charity ... Charity should make you a servant and free: a servant, because you have become such; free, because you are loved by God your Creator; indeed, you have also been enabled to love your Creator ... You are a servant of the Lord and you are a freedman of the Lord. Do not go looking for a liberation which will lead you far from the house of your liberator!" [140]

The Church, and each of her members, is thus called to share in the *munus regale* of the Crucified Christ (cf. *Jn* 12:32), to share in the grace and in the responsibility of the Son of man who came "not to be served but to serve, and to give his life as a ransom for many" (*Mt* 20:28).[141]

Jesus, then, is the living, personal summation of perfect freedom in total obedience to the will of God. His crucified flesh fully reveals the unbreakable bond between freedom and truth, just as his Resurrection from the dead is the supreme exaltation of the fruitfulness and saving power of a freedom lived out in truth.

Walking in the light (cf. *1 Jn* 1:7)

88.   The attempt to set freedom in opposition to truth, and indeed to separate them radically, is the consequence, manifestation and consum-

---

[140] *Enarratio in Psalmum XCIX*, 7: CCL 39, 1397.

[141] Cf. SECOND VATICAN ECUMENICAL COUNCIL, Dogmatic Constitution on the Church *Lumen Gentium*, 36; cf Encyclical Letter *Redemptor Hominis* (4 March 1979), 21: *AAS* 71 (1979), 316–317.

mation of *another more serious and destructive dichotomy, that which separates faith from morality*.

This separation represents one of the most acute pastoral concerns of the Church amid today's growing secularism, wherein many, indeed too many, people think and live "as if God did not exist". We are speaking of a mentality which affects, often in a profound, extensive and all-embracing way, even the attitudes and behaviour of Christians, whose faith is weakened and loses its character as a new and original criterion for thinking and acting in personal, family and social life. In a widely dechristianized culture, the criteria employed by believers themselves in making judgments and decisions often appear extraneous or even contrary to those of the Gospel.

It is urgent then that Christians should rediscover *the newness of the faith and its power to judge* a prevalent and all-intrusive culture. As the Apostle Paul admonishes us: "Once you were darkness, but now you are light in the Lord; walk as children of the light (for the fruit of the light is found in all that is good and right and true), and try to learn what is pleasing to the Lord. Take no part in the unfruitful words of darkness but instead expose them ... Look carefully then how you walk, not as unwise men but as wise, making the most of the time, because the days are evil" (*Eph* 5:8-11, 15-16; cf. *1 Th* 5:4-8).

It is urgent to redisover and to set forth once more the authentic reality of the Christian faith, which is not simply a set of propositions to be accepted with intellectual assent. Rather, faith is a lived knowledge of Christ, a living remembrance of his commandments, and a *truth to be lived out*. A word, in any event, is not truly received until it passes into action, until it is put into practice. Faith is a decision involving one's whole existence. It is an encounter, a dialogue, a communion of love and of life between the believer and Jesus Christ, the Way, and the Truth, and the Life (cf. *Jn* 14:6). It entails an act of trusting abandonment to Christ, which enables us to live as he lived (cf. *Gal* 2:20), in profound love of God and of our brothers and sisters.

89. Faith also possesses a moral content. It gives rise to and calls for a consistent life commitment; it entails and brings to perfection the acceptance and observance of God's commandments. As Saint John writes, "God is light and in him is no darkness at all. If we say we have fellowship with him while we walk in darkness, we lie and do not live according to the truth ... And by this we may be sure that we know him, if we keep his commandments. He who says 'I know him' but disobeys his commandments is a liar, and the truth is not in him; but whoever keeps his word, in him truly love for God is perfected. By this we may be sure that we are in him: he who says he abides in him ought to walk in the same way in which he walked"J(*1 Jn* 1:5–6; 2:3–6).

Through the moral life, faith becomes "confession", not only before God but also before men: it becomes *witness*. "You are the light of the world", said Jesus; "a city set on a hill cannot be hid. Nor do men light a lamp and put it under a bushel, but on a stand, and it gives light to all in the house. Let your light so shine before men, that they may see your good works and give glory to your Father who is in heaven" (*Mt* 5:14–16). These works are above all those of charity (cf. *Mt* 25:31–46) and of the authentic freedom which is manifested and lived in the gift of self, *even to the total gift of self*, like that of Jesus, who on the Cross "loved the Church and gave himself up for her" (*Eph* 5:25). Christ's witness is the source, model and means for the witness of his disciples, who are called to walk on the same road: "If any man would come after me, let him deny himself and take up his cross daily and follow me" (*Lk* 9:23). Charity, in conformity with the radical demands of the Gospel, can lead the believer to the supreme witness of *martyrdom*. Once again this means imitating Jesus who died on the Cross: "Be imitators of God, as beloved children", Paul writes to the Christians of Ephesus, "and walk in love, as Christ loved us and gave himself up for us, a fragrant offering and sacrifice to God" (*Eph* 5:1–2).

Martyrdom, the exaltation
of the inviolable holiness of God's law

90. The relationship between faith and morality shines forth with all its brilliance in the *unconditional respect due to the insistent demands of the personal dignity of every man*, demands protected by those moral norms which prohibit without exception actions which are intrinsically evil. The universality and the immutability of the moral norm make manifest and at the same time serve to protect the personal dignity and inviolability of man, on whose face is reflected the splendour of God (cf. *Gen* 9:5–6).

The unacceptability of "teleological", "consequentialist" and "proportionalist" ethical theories, which deny the existence of negative moral norms regarding specific kinds of behaviour, norms which are valid without exception, is confirmed in a particularly eloquent way by Christian martyrdom, which has always accompanied and continues to accompany the life of the Church even today.

91. In the Old Testament we already find admirable witnesses of fidelity to the holy law of God even to the point of a voluntary acceptance of death. A prime example is the story of Susanna: in reply to the two unjust judges who threatened to have her condemned to death if she refused to yield to their sinful passion, she says: "I am hemmed in on every side. For if I do this thing, it is death for me; and if I do not, I shall not escape your hands. I choose not to do it and to fall into your hands, rather than to sin in the sight of the Lord!" (*Dan* 13:22–23). Susanna, preferring to "fall innocent" into the hands of the judges, bears witness not only to her faith and trust in God but also to her obedience to the truth and to the absoluteness of the moral order. By her readiness to die a martyr, she proclaims that it is not right to do what God's law qualifies as evil in order to draw some good from it. Susanna chose for herself the "better part": hers was a perfectly clear witness, without any compromise, to the truth about the good and to the God of Israel. By her acts, she revealed the holiness of God.

At the dawn of the New Testament, *John the Baptist*, unable to refrain from speaking of the law of the Lord and rejecting any compromise with evil, "gave his life in witness to truth and justice",[142] and thus also became the forerunner of the Messiah in the way he died (cf. *Mk* 6:17–29). "The one who came to bear witness to the light and who deserved to be called by that same light, which is Christ, a burning and shining lamp, was cast into the darkness of prison ... The one to whom it was granted to baptize the Redeemer of the world was thus baptized in his own blood".[143]

In the New Testament we find many examples of *followers of Christ*, beginning with the deacon Stephen (cf. *Acts* 6:8—7:60) and the Apostle James (cf. *Acts* 12:1–2), who died as martyrs in order to profess their faith and their love for Christ, unwilling to deny him. In this they followed the Lord Jesus who "made the good confession" (*1 Tim* 6:13) before Caiaphas and Pilate, confirming the truth of his message at the cost of his life. Countless other martyrs accepted persecution and death rather than perform the idolatrous act of burning incense before the statue of the Emperor (cf. *Rev* 13:7–10). They even refused to feign such worship, thereby giving an example of the duty to refrain from performing even a single concrete act contrary to God's love and the witness of faith. Like Christ himself, they obediently trusted and handed over their lives to the Father, the one who could free them from death (cf. *Heb* 5:7).

The Church proposes the example of numerous Saints who bore

---

[142] *Roman Missal*, Prayer for the Memorial of the Beheading of John the Baptist, Martyr, August 29.
[143] Saint Bede the Venerable, *Homeliarum Evangelii Libri*, II, 23: CCL 122, 556–557.

witness to and defended moral truth even to the pint of enduring martyrdom, or who preferred death to a single mortal sin. In raising them to the honour of the altars, the Church has canonized their witness and declared the truth of their judgment, according to which the love of God entails the obligation to respect his commandments, even in the most dire of circumstances, and the refusal to betray those commandments, even for the sake of saving one's own life.

92.   Martyrdom, accepted as an affirmation of the inviolability of the moral order, bears splendid witness both to the holiness of God's law and to the inviolability of the personal dignity of man, created in God's image and likeness. This dignity may never be disparaged or called into question, even with good intentions, whatever the difficulties involved. Jesus warns us most sternly: "What does it profit a man, to gain the whole world and forfeit his life?" (Mk 8:36).

Martyrdom rejects as false and illusory whatever "human meaning" one might claim to attribute, even in "exceptional" conditions, to an act morally evil in itself. Indeed, it even more clearly unmasks the true face of such an act: it is a violation of man's "humanity", in the one perpetrating it even before the one enduring it.[144] Hence martyrdom is also the exaltation of a person's perfect "humanity" and of true "life", as is attested by Saint Ignatius of Antioch, addressing the Christians of Rome, the place of his own martyrdom: "Have mercy on me, brethren: do not hold me back from living; do not wish that I die ... Let me arrive at the pure light; once there I will be truly a man. Let me imitate the passion of my God".[145]

93.   Finally, martyrdom is an outstanding sign of the holiness of the Church. Fidelity to God's holy law, witnessed to by death, is a solemn proclamation and missionary commitment usque ad sanguinem, so that the splendour of moral truth may be undimmed in the behaviour and thinking of individuals and society. This witness makes an extraordinarily valuable contribution to warding off, in civil society and within the ecclesial communities themselves, a headlong plunge into the most dangerous crisis which can afflict man: the confusion between good and evil, which makes it impossible to build up and to preserve the moral order of individuals and communities. By their eloquent and attractive example of a life completely transfigured by the splendour of moral truth, the martyrs and, in general, all the Church's Saints, light up every period of

[144] Cf. SECOND VATICAN ECUMENICAL COUNCIL, Pastoral Constitution on the Church in the Modern World Gaudium et Spes, 27.
[145] Ad Romanos, VI, 2–3: Patres Apostolici, ed. F.X. FUNK, I, 260–261.

history by reawakening its moral sense. By witnessing fully to the good, they are a living reproof to those who transgress the law (cf. *Wis* 2:12), and they make the words of the Prophet echo ever afresh: "Woe to those who call evil good and good evil, who put darkness for light and light for darkness, who put bitter for sweet and sweet for bitter!" (*Is* 5:20).

Although martyrdom represents the high point of the witness to moral truth, and one to which relatively few people are called, there is nonetheless a consistent witness which all Christians must daily be ready to make, even at the cost of suffering and grave sacrifice. Indeed, faced with the many difficulties which fidelity to the moral order can demand, even in the most ordinary circumstances, the Christian is called, with the grace of God invoked in prayer, to a sometimes heroic commitment. In this he or she is sustained by the virtue of fortitude, whereby—as Gregory the Great teaches—one can actually "love the difficulties of this world for the sake of eternal rewards".[146]

94. In this witness to the absoluteness of the moral good *Christians are not alone*: they are supported by the moral sense present in peoples and by the great religious and sapiential traditions of East and West, from which the interior and mysterious workings of God's Spirit are not absent. The words of the Latin poet Juvenal apply to all: "Consider it the greatest of crimes to prefer survival to honour and, out of love of physical life, to lose the very reason for living".[147] The voice of conscience has always clearly recalled that there are truths and moral values for which one must be prepared to give up one's life. In an individual's words and above all in the sacrifice of his life for a moral value, the Church sees a single testimony to that truth which, already present in creation, shines forth in its fullness on the face of Christ. As Saint Justin put it, "the Stoics, at least in their teachings on ethics, demonstrated wisdom, thanks to the seed of the Word present in all peoples, and we know that those who followed their doctrines met with hatred and were killed".[148]

---

[146] *Moralia in Job*, VII, 21, 24: *PL* 75, 778: "huius mundi aspera pro aeternis praemiis amare".

[147] "Summum crede nefas ánimam praeferre pudori et propter vitam vivendi perdere causas": *Satirae*, VIII, 83–84.

[148] *Apologia* II, 8: *PG* 6, 457–458.

Universal and unchanging moral norms
at the service of the person and of society

95. The Church's teaching, and in particular her firmness in defending the universal and permanent validity of the precepts prohibiting intrinsically evil acts, is not infrequently seen as the sign of an intolerable intransigence, particularly with regard to the enormously complex and conflict-filled situations present in the moral life of individuals and of society today; this intransigence is said to be in contrast with the Church's motherhood. The Church, one hears, is lacking in understanding and compassion. But the Church's motherhood can never in fact be separated from her teaching mission, which she must always carry out as the faithful Bride of Christ, who is the Truth in person. "As Teacher, she never tires of proclaiming the moral norm ... The Church is in no way the author or the arbiter of this norm. In obedience to the truth which is Christ, whose image is reflected in the nature and dignity of the human person, the Church interprets the moral norm and proposes it to all people of good will, without concealing its demands of radicalness and perfection".[149]

In fact, genuine understanding and compassion must mean love for the person, for his true good, for his authentic freedom And this does not result, certainly, from concealing or weakening moral truth, but rather from proposing it in its most profound meaning as an outpouring of God's eternal Wisdom, which we have received in Christ, and as a service to man, to the growth of his freedom and to the attainment of his happiness.[150]

Still, a clear and forceful presentation of moral truth can never be separated from a profound and heartfelt respect, born of that patient and trusting love which man always needs along his moral journey, a journey frequently wearisome on account of difficulties, weakness and painful situations. The Church can never renounce the "the principle of truth and consistency, whereby she does not agree to call good evil and evil good";[151] she must always be careful not to break the bruised reed or to quench the dimly burning wick (cf. *Is* 42:3). As Paul VI wrote: "While it is an outstanding manifestation of charity towards souls to omit nothing from the saving doctrine of Christ, this must always be joined with

---

[149] Apostolic Exhortation *Familiaris Consortio* (22 November 1981), 33: *AAS* 74 (1982), 120.

[150] Cf. *ibid.*, 34: *loc. cit.*, 123–125.

[151] Post-Synodal Apostolic Exhortation *Reconciliatio et Paenitentia* (2 December 1984), 34: *AAS* 77 (1985), 272.

tolerance and charity, as Christ himself showed by his conversations and dealings with men. Having come not to judge the world but to save it, he was uncompromisingly stern towards sin, but patient and rich in mercy towards sinners".[152]

96.   The Church's firmness in defending the universal and unchanging moral norms is not demeaning at all. Its only purpose is to serve man's true freedom. Because there can be no freedom apart from or in opposition to the truth, the categorical—unyielding and uncompromising—defence of the absolutely essential demands of man's personal dignity must be considered the way and the condition for the very existence of freedom.

This service is directed to *every man*, considered in the uniqueness and singularity of his being and existence: only by obedience to universal moral norms does man find full confirmation of his pesonal uniqueness and the possibility of authentic moral growth. For this very reason, this service is also directed to *all mankind*: it is not only for individuals but also for the community, for society as such. These norms in fact represent the unshakable foundation and solid guarantee of a just and peaceful human coexistence, and hence of genuine democracy, which can come into being and develop only on the basis of the equality of all its members, who possess common rights and duties. *When it is a matter of the moral norms prohibiting intrinsic evil, there are no privileges or exceptions for anyone.* It makes no difference whether one is the master of the world or the "poorest of the poor" on the face of the earth. Before the demands of morality we are all absolutely equal.

97.   In this way, moral norms, and primarily the negative ones, those prohibiting evil, manifest their *meaning and force, both personal and social.* By protecting the inviolable personal dignity of every human being they help to preserve the human social fabric and its proper and fruitful development. The commandments of the second table of the Decalogue in particular—those which Jesus quoted to the young man of the Gospel (cf. *Mt* 19:19)—constitute the indispensable rules of all social life.

These commandments are formulated in general terms. But the very fact that "the origin, the subject and the purpose of all social institutions is and should be the human person"[153] allows for them to be specified and made more explicit in a detailed code of behaviour. The fundamental

---

[152] Encyclical Letter *Humanae Vitae* (25 July 1968), 29: *AAS* 60 (1968), 501.
[153] SECOND VATICAN ECUMENICAL COUNCIL, Pastoral Constitution on the Church in the Modern World *Gaudium et Spes*, 25.

moral rules of social life thus entail *specific demands* to which both public authorities and citizens are required to pay heed. Even though intentions may sometimes be good, and circumstances frequently difficult, civil authorities and particular individuals never have authority to violate the fundamental and inalienable rights of the human person. In the end, only a morality which acknowledges certain norms as valid always and for everyone, with no exception, can guarantee the ethical foundation of social coexistence, both on the national and international levels.

Morality and the renewal of social and political life

98. In the face of serious forms of social and economic injustice and political corruption affecting entire peoples and nations, there is a growing reaction of indignation on the part of very many people whose fundamental human rights have been trampled upon and held in contempt, as well as an ever more widespread and acute sense of *the need for a radical* personal and social *renewal* capable of ensuring justice, solidarity, honesty and openness.

Certainly there is a long and difficult road ahead; bringing about such a renewal will require enormous effort, especially on account of the number and the gravity of the causes giving rise to and aggravating the situations of injustice present in the world today. But, as history and personal experience show, it is not difficult to discover at the bottom of these situations causes which are properly "cultural", linked to particular ways of looking at man, society and the world. Indeed, at the heart of the issue of culture we find the *moral sense*, which is in turn rooted and fulfilled in the *religious sense*.[154]

99. Only God, the Supreme Good, constitutes the unshakable foundation and essential condition of morality, and thus of the commandments, particularly those negative commandments which always and in every case prohibit behaviour and actions incompatible with the personal dignity of every man. The Supreme Good and the moral good meet in *truth*: the truth of God, the Creator and Redeemer, and the truth of man, created and redeemed by him. Only upon this truth is it possible to construct a renewed society and to solve the complex and weighty problems affecting it, above all the problem of overcoming the various

---

[154] Cf. Encyclical Letter *Centesimus Annus* (1 May 1991), 24: *AAS* 83 (1991), 821–822.

forms of totalitarianism, so as to make way for the authentic *freedom* of the person. "Totalitarianism arises out of a denial of truth in the objective sense. If there is no transcendent truth, in obedience to which man achieves his full identity, then there is no sure principle for guaranteeing just relations between people. Their self-interest as a class, group or nation would inevitably set them in opposition to one another. If one does not acknowledge transcendent truth, then the force of power takes over, and each person tends to make full use of the means at his disposal in order to impose his own interests or his own opinion, with no regard for the rights of others ... Thus, the root of modern totalitarianism is to be found in the denial of the transcendent dignity of the human person who, as the visible image of the invisible God, is therefore by his very nature the subject of rights which no one may violate—no individual, group, class, nation or State. Not even the majority of a social body may violate these rights, by going against the minority, by isolating, oppressing, or exploiting it, or by attempting to annihilate it".[155]

Consequently, the inseparable connection between truth and freedom—which expresses the essential bond between God's wisdom and will—is extremely significant for the life of persons in the socio-economic and socio-political sphere. This is clearly seen in the Church's social teaching—which "belongs to the field ... of theology and particularly of moral theology"[156]—and from her presentation of commandments governing social, economic and political life, not only with regard to general attitudes but also to precise and specific kinds of behaviour and concrete acts.

100. The *Catechism of the Catholic Church* affirms that "in economic matters, respect for human dignity requires the practice of the virtue of *temperance*, to moderate our attachment to the goods of this world; of the virtue of *justice*, to preserve our neighbour's rights and to render what is his or her due; and of *solidarity*, following the Golden Rule and in keeping with the generosity of the Lord, who 'though he was rich, yet for your sake ... became poor, so that by his poverty you might become rich' (*2 Cor* 8:9)".[157] The Catechism goes on to present a series of kinds of behaviour and actions contrary to human dignity: theft, deliberate retention of goods lent or objects lost, business fraud (cf. *Dt* 25:13–16), unjust wages (cf. *Dt* 24:14–15), forcing up prices by trading on the

---

[155] *Ibid.*, 44: *loc. cit.*, 848—849; cf. Leo XIII, Encyclical Letter *Libertas Praestantissimum* (20 June 1888): *Leonis XIII P.M. Acta*, VIII, Romae 1889, 224–226.

[156] Encyclical Letter *Sollicitudo Rei Socialis* (30 December 1987), 41: *AAS* 80 (1988), 571.

[157] *Catechism of the Catholic Church*, No. 2407.

ignorance or hardship of another (cf. *Am* 8:4–6), the misappropriation and private use of the corporate property of an enterprise, work badly done, tax fraud, forgery of cheques and invoices, excessive expenses, waste, etc.[158] It continues: "The seventh commandment prohibits actions or enterprises which for any reason—selfish or ideological, commercial or totalitarian—lead to the *enslavement of human beings*, disregard for their personal dignity, buying or selling or exchanging them like merchandise. Reducing persons by violence to use-value or a source of profit is a sin against their dignity as persons and their fundamental rights. Saint Paul set a Christian master right about treating his Christian slave 'no longer as a slave but . . . as a brother . . . in the Lord' (*Philem* 16)".[159]

101. In the political sphere, it must be noted that truthfulness in the relations between those governing and those governed, openness in public administration, impartiality in the service of the body politic, respect for the rights of political adversaries, safeguarding the rights of the accused against summary trials and convictions, the just and honest use of public funds, the rejection of equivocal or illicit means in order to gain, preserve or increase power at any cost—all these are principles which are primarily rooted in, and in fact derive their singular urgency from, the transcendent value of the person and the objective moral demands of the functioning of States.[160] When these principles are not observed, the very basis of political coexistence is weakened and the life of society itself is gradually jeopardized, threatened and doomed to decay (cf. *Ps* 14:3–4; *Rev* 18:2–3, 9–24). Today, when many countries have seen the fall of ideologies which bound politics to a totalitarian conception of the world—Marxism being the foremost of these—there is no less grave a danger that the fundamental rights of the human person will be denied and that the religious yearnings which arise in the heart of every human being will be asborbed once again into politics. This is *the risk of an alliance between democracy and ethical relativism*, which would remove any sure moral reference point from political and social life, and on a deeper level make the acknowledgement of truth impossible. Indeed, "if there is no ultimate truth to guide and direct political activity, then ideas and convictions can easily be manipulated for reasons of power. As history demonstrates, a democracy without values easily turns into open or thinly disguised totalitarianism".[161]

---

[158] Cf. *ibid.*, Nos. 2408–2413.

[159] *Ibid.*, No. 2414.

[160] Cf. Encyclical Letter *Christifideles Laici* (30 December 1988), 42: *AAS* 81 (1989), 472–476.

[161] Encyclical Letter *Centesimus Annus* (1 May 1991), 46: *AAS* 83 (1991), 850.

Thus, in every sphere of personal, family, social and political life, morality—founded upon truth and open in truth to authentic freedom—renders a primordial, indispensable and immensely valuable service not only for the individual person and his growth in the good, but also for society and its genuine development.

Grace and obedience to God's law

102. Even in the most difficult situations man must respect the norm of morality so that he can be obedient to God's holy commandment and consistent with his own dignity as a person. Certainly, maintaining a harmony between freedom and truth occasionally demands uncommon sacrifices, and must be won at a high price: it can even involve martyrdom. But, as universal and daily experience demonstrates, man is tempted to break that harmony: "I do not do what I want, but I do the very thing I hate ... I do not do the good I want, but the evil I do not want" (*Rom* 7:15, 19).

What is the ultimate source of this inner division of man? His history of sin begins when he no longer acknowledges the Lord as his Creator and himself wishes to be the one who determines, with complete independence, what is good and what is evil. "You will be like God, knowing good and evil" (*Gen* 3:5): this was the first temptation, and it is echoed in all the other temptations to which man is more easily inclined to yield as a result of the original Fall.

But temptations can be overcome, sins can be avoided, because together with the commandments the Lord gives us the possibility of keeping them: "His eyes are on those who fear him, and he knows every deed of man. He has not commanded any one to be ungodly, and he has not given any one permission to sin" (*Sir* 15:19–20). Keeping God's law in particular situations can be difficult, extremely difficult, but it is never impossible. This is the constant teaching of the Church's tradition, and was expressed by the Council of Trent: "But no one, however much justified, ought to consider himself exempt from the observance of the commandments, nor should he employ that rash statement, forbidden by the Fathers under anathema, that the commandments of God are impossible of observance by one who is justified. For God does not command the impossible, but in commanding he admonishes you to do what you can and to pray for what you cannot, and he gives his aid to enable you. His commandments are not burdensome (cf. *1 Jn* 5:3); his yoke is easy and his burden light (cf. *Mt* 11:30)".[162]

---

[162] Sess. VI, Decree on Justification *Cum Hoc Tempore*, Chap. 11: *DS*, 1536; cf. Canon 18: *DS*, 1568. The celebrated text from Saint Augustine, which the Council cites, is found in *De Natura et Gratia*, 43, 40 (*CSEL* 60, 270).

103.   Man always has before him the spiritual horizon of hope, thanks to the *help of divine grace* and with *the cooperation of human freedom*.

It is in the saving Cross of Jesus, in the gift of the Holy Spirit, in the Sacraments which flow forth from the pierced side of the Redeemer (cf. Jn 19:34), that believers find the grace and the strength always to keep God's holy law, even amid the gravest of hardships. As Saint Andrew of Crete observes, the law itself "was enlivened by grace and made to serve it in a harmonious and fruitful combination. Each element preserved its characteristics without change or confusion. In a divine manner, he turned what could be burdensome and tyrannical into what is easy to bear and a source of freedom".[163]

Only in the mystery of Christ's Redemption do we discover the "concrete" possibilities of man. "It would be a very serious error to conclude . . . that the Church's teaching is essentially only an 'ideal' which must then be adapted, proportioned, graduated to the so-called concrete possibilities of man, according to a 'balancing of the goods in question'. But what are the 'concrete possibilities of man'? And of *which* man are we speaking? Of man *dominated* by lust or of man *redeemed by Christ?* This is what is at stake: the *reality* of Christ's redemption. *Christ has redeemed us!* This means that he has given us the possibility of realizing *the entire* truth of our being; he has set our freedom free from the *domination* of concupiscence. And if redeemed man still sins, this is not due to an imperfection of Christ's redemptive act, but to man's will not to avail himself of the grace which flows from that act. God's command is of course proportioned to man's capabilities; but to the capabilities of the man to whom the Holy Spirit has been given; of the man who, though he has fallen into sin, can always obtain pardon and enjoy the presence of the Holy Spirit".[164]

104.   In this context, appropriate allowance is made both for *God's mercy* towards the sin of the man who experiences conversion and for the *understanding of human weakness*. Such understanding never means compromising and falsifying the standard of good and evil in order to adapt it to particular circumstances. It is quite human for the sinner to acknowledge his weakness and to ask mercy for his failings; what is unacceptable is the attitude of one who makes his own weakness the criterion of the truth about the good, so that he can feel self-justified, without even the need to have recourse to God and his mercy. An attitude of this sort corrupts the morality of society as a whole, since it encourages doubt about the

---

[163] *Oratio* I: *PG* 97, 805–806.

[164] *Address* to those taking part in a course on "responsible parenthood" (1 March 1984), 4: *Insegnamenti* VII, 1 (1984), 583.

objectivity of the moral law in general and a rejection of the absoluteness of moral prohibitions regarding specific human acts, and it ends up by confusing all judgments about values.

Instead, we should take to heart the *message of the Gospel parable of the Pharisee and the tax collector* (cf. *Lk* 18:9–14). The tax collector might possibly have had some justification for the sins he committed, such as to dimish his responsibility. But his prayer does not dwell on such justifications, but rather on his own unworthiness before God's infinite holiness: "God, be merciful to me a sinner!" (*Lk* 18:13). The Pharisee, on the other hand, is self-justified, finding some excuse for each of his failings. Here we encounter two different attitudes of the moral conscience of man in every age. The tax collector represents a "repentant" conscience, fully aware of the frailty of its own nature and seeing in its own failings, whatever their subjective justifications, a confirmation of its need for redemption. The Pharisee represents a "self-satisfied" conscience, under the illusion that it is able to observe the law without the help of grace and convinced that it does not need mercy.

105. All people must take great care not to allow themselves to be tainted by the attitude of the Pharisee, which would seek to eliminate awareness of one's own limits and of one's own sin. In our own day this attitude is expressed particularly in the attempt to adapt the moral norm to one's own capacities and personal interests, and even in the rejection of the very idea of a norm. Accepting, on the other hand, the "disproportion" between the law and human ability (that is, the capacity of the moral forces of man left to himself) kindles the desire for grace and prepares one to receive it. "Who will deliver me from this body of death?" asks the Apostle Paul. And in an outburst of joy and gratitude he replies: "Thanks be to God through Jesus Christ our Lord!" (*Rom* 7:24–25).

We find the same awareness in the following prayer of Saint Ambrose of Milan: "What then is man, if you do not visit him? Remember, Lord, that you have made me as one who is weak, that you formed me from dust. How can I stand, if you do not constantly look upon me, to strengthen this clay, so that my strength may proceed from your face? *When you hide your face, all grows weak* (*Ps* 104:29): if you turn to look at me, woe is me! You have nothing to see in me but the stain of my crimes; there is no gain either in being abandoned or in being seen, because when we are seen, we offend you. Still, we can imagine that God does not reject those he sees, because he purifies those upon whom he gazes. Before him burns a fire capable of consuming our guilt (cf. *Joel* 2:3)".[165]

---

[165] *De Interpellatione David*, IV, 6, 22: CSEL 32/2, 283–284.

Morality and new evangelization

106. Evangelization is the most powerful and stirring challenge which the Church has been called to face from her very beginning. Indeed, this challenge is posed not so much by the social and cultural milieux which she encounters in the course of history, as by the mandate of the Risen Christ, who defines the very reason for the Church's existence: "Go into all the world and preach the Gospel to the whole creation" (*Mk* 16:15).

At least for many peoples, however, the present time is instead marked by a formidable challenge to undertake a "new evangelization", a proclamation of the Gospel which is always new and always the bearer of new things, an evangelization which must be "new in its ardour, methods and expression".[166] Dechristianization, which weighs heavily upon entire peoples and communities once rich in faith and Christian life, involves not only the loss of faith or in any event its becoming irrelevant for everyday life, but also, and of necessity, *a decline or obscuring of the moral sense*. This comes about both as a result of a loss of awareness of the originality of Gospel morality and as a result of an eclipse of fundamental principles and ethical values themselves. Today's widespread tendencies towards subjectivism, utilitarianism and relativism appear not merely as pragmatic attitudes or patterns of behaviour, but rather as approaches having a basis in theory and claiming full cultural and social legitimacy.

107. *Evangelization*—and therefore the "new evangelization"—*also involves the proclamation and presentation of morality*. Jesus himself, even as he preached the Kingdom of God and its saving love, called people to faith and conversion (cf. *Mk* 1:15). And when Peter, with the other Apostles, proclaimed the Resurrection of Jesus of Nazareth from the dead, he held out a new life to be lived, a "way" to be followed, for those who would be disciples of the Risen One (cf. *Acts* 2:37–41; 3:17–20).

Just as it does in proclaiming the truths of faith, and even more so in presenting the foundations and content of Christian morality, the new evangelization will shows its authenticity and unleash all its missionary force when it is carried out through the gift not only of the word proclaimed but also of the word lived. In particular, *the life of holiness* which is resplendent in so many members of the People of God, humble

---

[166] *Address* to the Bishops of CELAM (9 March 1983), III: *Insegnamenti*, VI, 1 (1983), 698.

and often unseen, constitutes the simplest and most attractive way to perceive at once the beauty of truth, the liberating force of God's love, and the value of unconditional fidelity to all the demands of the Lord's law, even in the most difficult situations. For this reason, the Church, as a wise teacher or morality, has always invited believers to seek and to find in the Saints, and above all in the Virgin Mother of God "full of grace" and "all-holy", the model, the strength and the joy needed to live a life in accordance with God's commandments and the Beatitudes of the Gospel.

The lives of the saints, as a reflection of the goodness of God—the One who "alone is good"—constitute not only a genuine profession of faith and an incentive for sharing it with others, but also a glorification of God and his infinite holiness. The life of holiness thus brings to full expression and effectiveness the three-fold and unitary *munus propheticum, sacerdotale et regale* which every Christian receives as a gift of being born again "of water and the Spirit" (*Jn* 3:5) in Baptism. His moral life has the value of a "spiritual worship" (*Rom* 12:1; cf. *Phil* 3:3), flowing from and nourished by that inexhaustible source of holiness and glorification of God which is found in the Sacraments, especially in the Eucharist: by sharing in the sacrifice of the Cross, the Christian partakes of Christ's self-giving love and is equipped and committed to live this same charity in all his thoughts and deeds. In the moral life the Christian's royal service is also made evident and effective: with the help of grace, the more one obeys the new law of the Holy Spirit, the more one grows in the freedom to which he or she is called by the service of truth, charity and justice.

108. At the heart of the new envangelization and of the new moral life which it proposes and awakens by its fruits of holiness and missionary zeal, there is *the Spirit of Christ*, the principle and strength of the fruitfulness of Holy Mother Church. As Pope Paul VI reminded us: "Evangelization will never be possible without the action of the Holy Spirit".[167] The Spirit of Jesus, received by the humble and docile heart of the believer, brings about the flourishing of Christian moral life and the witness of holiness amid the great variety of vocations, gifts, responsibilities, conditions and life situations. As Novatian once pointed out, here expressing the authentic faith of the Church, it is the Holy Spirit "who confirmed the hearts and minds of the disciples, who revealed the mysteries of the Gospel, who shed upon them the light of things divine. Strengthened by his gift, they did not fear either prisons or chains for the

---

[167] Apostolic Exhortation *Evangelii Nuntiandi* (8 December 1975), 75: *AAS* 68 (1976), 64.

name of the Lord; indeed they even trampled upon the powers and torments of the world, armed and strengthened by him, having in themselves the gifts which this same Spirit bestows and directs like jewels to the Church, the Bride of Christ. It is in fact he who raises up prophets in the Church, instructs teachers, guides tongues, works wonders and healings, accomplishes miracles, grants the discernment of spirits, assigns governance, inspires counsels, distributes and harmonizes every other charismatic gift. In this way he completes and perfects the Lord's Church everywhere and in all things".[168]

In the living context of this new evangelization, aimed at generating and nourishing "the faith which works through love" (cf. *Gal* 5:6), and in relation to the work of the Holy Spirit, we can now understand the proper place which *continuing theological reflection about the moral life* holds in the Church, the community of believers. We can likewise speak of the mission and the responsibility proper to moral theologians.

The service of moral theologians

109. The whole Church is called to evangelization and to the witness of a life of faith, by the fact that she has been made a sharer in the *munus propheticum* of the Lord Jesus through the gift of his Spirit. Thanks to the permanent presence of the Spirit of truth in the Church (cf. *Jn* 14:16–17), "the universal body of the faithful who have received the anointing of the holy one (cf. *1 Jn* 2:20, 27) cannot be mistaken in belief. It displays this particular quality through a supernatural sense of the faith in the whole people when, 'from the Bishops to the last of the lay faithful', it expresses the consensus of all in matters of faith and morals".[169]

In order to carry out her prophetic mission, the Church must constantly reawaken or "rekindle" her own life of faith (cf. *2 Tim* 1:6), particularly through an ever deeper reflection, under the guidance of the Holy Spirit, upon the content of faith itself. *The "vocation" of the theologian in the Church* is specifically at the service of this "believing effort to understand the faith". As the Instruction *Donum Veritatis* teaches: "Among the vocations awakened by the Spirit in the Church is that of the theologian. His role is to pursue in a particular way an ever deeper understanding of the word of God found in the inspired Scriptures and handed on by the living Tradition of the Church. He does this in communion with the Magisterium, which has been charged with the

---

[168] *De Trinitate*, XXIX, 9–10: CCL 4, 70.
[169] SECOND VATICAN ECUMENICAL COUNCIL, Dogmatic Constitution on the Church *Lumen Gentium*, 12.

responsibility of preserving the deposit of faith. By its nature, faith appeals to reason because it reveals to man the truth of his destiny and the way to attain it. Revealed truth, to be sure, surpasses our telling. All our concepts fall short of its ultimately unfathomable grandeur (cf. *Eph* 3:19). Nonetheless, revealed truth beckons reason—God's gift fashioned for the assimilation of truth—to enter into its light and thereby come to understand in a certain measure what it has believed. Theological science responds to the invitation of truth as it seeks to understand the faith. It thereby aids the People of God in fulfilling the Apostle's command (cf. *1 Pet* 3:15) to give an accounting for their hope to those who ask it".[170]

It is fundamental for defining the very identity of theology, and consequently for theology to carry out its proper mission, to recognize its *profound and vital connection with the Church, her mystery, her life and her mission:* "Theology is an ecclesial science because it grows in the Church and works on the Church ... It is a service to the Church and therefore ought to feel itself actively involved in the mission of the Church, particularly in its prophetic mission".[171] By its very nature and procedures, authentic theology can flourish and develop only through a committed and responsible participation in and "belonging" to the Church as a "community of faith". In turn, the fruits of theological research and deeper insight become a source of enrichment for the Church and her life of faith.

110.   All that has been said about theology in general can and must also be said for *moral theology*, seen in its specific nature as a scientific reflection on the *Gospel as the gift and commandment of new life*, a reflection on the life which "professes the truth in love" (cf. *Eph* 4:15) and on the Church's life of holiness, in which there shines forth the truth about the good brought to its perfection. The Church's Magisterium intervenes not only in the sphere of faith, but also, and inseparably so, in the sphere of morals. It has the task of "discerning, by means of judgments normative for the consciences of believers, those acts which in themselves conform to the demands of faith and foster their expression in life and those which, on the contrary, because intrinsically evil, are incompatible with such demands".[172] In proclaiming the commandments of God and the charity of Christ, the Church's Magisterium also teaches the faithful specific particular precepts and requires that they consider them in

---

[170] CONGREGATION FOR THE DOCTRINE OF THE FAITH, Instruction on the Ecclesial Vocation of the Theologian *Donum Veritatis* (24 May 1990), 6: *AAS* 82 (1990), 1552.

[171] *Address* to the Professors and Students of the Pontifical Gregorian University (15 December 1979), 6: *Insegnamenti* II, 2 (1979), 1424.

[172] CONGREGATION FOR THE DOTRINE OF THE FAITH, Instruction on the Ecclesial Vocation of the Theologian *Donum Veritatis* (24 May 1990), 16: *AAS* 82 (1990), 1557.

conscience as morally binding. In addition, the Magisterium carries out an important work of vigilance, warning the faithful of the presence of possible errors, even merely implicit ones, when their consciences fail to acknowledge the correctness and the truth of the moral norms which the Magisterium teaches.

This is the point at which to consider the specific task of all those who by mandate of their legitimate Pastors teach moral theology in Seminaries and Faculties of Theology. They have the grave duty to instruct the faithful—especially future Pastors—about all those commandments and practical norms authoritatively declared by the Church.[173] While recognizing the possible limitations of the human arguments employed by the Magisterium, moral theologians are called to develop a deeper understnding of the reasons underlying its teachings and to expound the validity and obligatory nature of the precepts it proposes, demonstrating their connection with one another and their relation with man's ultimate end.[174] Moral theologians are to set forth the Church's teaching and to give, in the exercise of their ministry, the example of a loyal assent, both internal and external, to the Magisterium's teaching in the areas of both dogma and morality.[175] Working together in cooperation with the hierarchical Magisterium, theologians will be deeply concerned to clarify ever more fully the biblical foundations, the ethical significance and the anthropological concerns which underlie the moral doctrine and the vision of man set forth by the Church.

III. The service which moral theologians are called to provide at the present time is of the utmost importance, not only for the Church's life and mission, but also for human society and culture. Moral theologians have the task, in close and vital connection with biblical and dogmatic theology, to highlight through their scientific reflection "that dynamic aspect which will elicit the response that man must give to the divine call which comes in the process of his growth in love, within a community of salvation. In this way, moral theology will acquire an inner spiritual dimension in response to the need to develop fully the *imago Dei* present in man, and in response to the laws of spiritual development described by Christian ascetical and mystical theology".[176]

---

[173] Cf. *Code of Canon Law*, Canons 252, 1; 659, 3.

[174] Cf. FIRST VATICAN ECUMENICAL COUNCIL, Dogmatic Constitution on the Catholic Faith *Dei Filius*, Chap. 4: *DS*, 3016.

[175] Cf. PAUL VI, Encyclical Letter *Humanae Vitae* (25 July 1968), 28: *AAS* 60 (1968), 501.

176 SACRED CONGREGATION FOR CATHOLIC EDUCATION, *The Theological Formation of Future Priests* (22 February 1976), No. 100. See Nos. 95–101, which present the prospects and conditions for a fruitful renewal of moral theology: *loc. cit.*, 39–41.

Certainly moral theology and its teaching are meeting with particular difficulty today. Because the Church's morality necessarily involves a *normative* dimension, moral theology cannot be reduced to a body of knowledge worked out purely in the context of the so-called *behavioural sciences*. The latter are concerned with the phenomenon of morality as a historical and social fact; moral theology, however, while needing to make use of the behavioural and natural sciences, does not rely on the results of formal empirical observation or phenomenological understanding alone. Indeed, the relevance of the behavioural sciences for moral theology must always be measured against the primordial question: *What is good or evil? What must be done to have eternal life?*

112. The moral theologian must therefore exercise careful discernment in the context of today's prevalently scientific and technical culture, exposed as it is to the dangers of relativism, pragmatism and positivism. From the theological viewpoint, moral principles are not dependent upon the historical moment in which they are discovered. Moreover, the fact that some believers act without following the teachings of the Magisterium, or erroneously consider as morally correct a kind of behaviour declared by their Pastors as contrary to the law of God, cannot be a valid argument for rejecting the truth of the moral norms taught by the Church. The affirmation of moral principles is not within the competence of formal empirical methods. While not denying the validity of such methods, but at the same time not restricting its viewpoint to them, moral theology, faithful to the supernatural sense of the faith, takes into account first and foremost *the spiritual dimension of the human heart and its vocation to divine love.*

In fact, while the behavioural sciences, like all experimental sciences, develop an empirical and statistical concept of "normality", faith teaches that this normality itself bears the traces of a fall from man's original situation—in other words, it is affected by sin. Only Christian faith points out to man the way to return to "the beginning" (cf. *Mt* 19:8), a way which is often quite different from that of empirical normality. Hence the behavioural sciences, despite the great value of the information which they provide, cannot be considered decisive indications of moral norms. It is the Gospel which reveals the full truth about man and his moral journey, and thus enlightens and admonishes sinners; it proclaims to them God's mercy, which is constantly at work to preserve them both from despair at their inability fully to know and keep God's law and from the presumption that they can be saved without merit. God also reminds sinners of the joy of forgiveness, which alone grants the strength to see in the moral law a liberating truth, a grace-filled source of hope, a path of life.

113. Teaching moral doctrine involves the conscious acceptance of these intellectual, spiritual and pastoral responsibilities. Moral theologians, who have accepted the charge of teaching the Church's doctrine, thus have a grave duty to train the faithful to make this moral discernment, to be committed to the true good and to have confident recourse to God's grace.

While exchanges and conflicts of opinion may constitute normal expressions of public life in a respresentative democracy, moral teaching certainly cannot depend simply upon respect for a process: indeed, it is in no way established by following the rules and deliberative procedures typical of a democracy. *Dissent*, in the form of carefully orchestrated protests and polemics carried on in the media, *is opposed to ecclesial communion and to a correct understanding of the hierarchical constitution of the People of God.* Opposition to the teaching of the Church's Pastors cannot be seen as a legitimate expression either of Christian freedom or of the diversity of the Spirit's gifts. When this happens, the Church's Pastors have the duty of act in conformity with their apostolic mission, insisting that *the right of the faithful* to receive Catholic doctrine in its purity and integrity must always be respected. "Never forgetting that he too is a member of the People of God, the theologian must be respectful of them, and be committed to offering them a teaching which in no way does harm to the doctrine of the faith".[177]

Our own responsibilities as Pastors

114. As the Second Vatican Council reminds us, responsibility for the faith and the life of faith of the People of God is particularly incumbent upon the Church's Pastors: "Among the principal tasks of Bishops the preaching of the Gospel is pre-eminent. For the Bishops are the heralds of the faith who bring new disciples to Christ. They are authentic teachers, that is, teachers endowed with the authority of Christ, who preach to the people entrusted to them the faith to be believed and put into practice; they illustrate this faith in the light of the Holy Spirit, drawing out of the treasury of Revelation things old and new (cf. *Mt* 13:52); they make it bear fruit and they vigilantly ward off errors that are threatening their flock (cf. *2 Tim* 4:1–4)".[178]

It is our common duty, and even before that our common grace, as

---

[177] CONGREGATION FOR THE DOCTRINE OF THE FAITH, Instruction on the Ecclesial Vocation of the Theologian *Donum Veritatis* (24 May 1990), 11: *AAS* 82 (1990), 1554; cf. in particular Nos. 32–39, devoted to the problem of dissent: *ibid., loc. cit.,* 1562–1568.

[178] Dogmatic Constitution on the Church *Lumen Gentium*, 25.

Pastors and Bishops of the Church, to teach the faithful the things which lead them to God, just as the Lord Jesus did with the young man in the Gospel. Replying to the question: "What good must I do to have eternal life?", Jesus referred the young man to God, the Lord of creation and of the Covenant. He reminded him of the moral commandments already revealed in the Old Testament and he indicated their spirit and deepest meaning by inviting the young man to follow him in poverty, humility and love: "Come, follow me!" The truth of this teaching was sealed on the Cross in the Blood of Christ: in the Holy Spirit, it has become the new law of the Church and of every Christian.

This "answer" to the question about morality has been entrusted by Jesus Christ in a particular way to us, the Pastors of the Church; we have been called to make it the object of our preaching, in the fulfilment of our *munus propheticum*. At the same time, our responsibility as Pastors with regard to Christian moral teaching must also be exercised as part of the *munus sacerdotale:* this happens when we dispense to the faithful the gifts of grace and sanctification as an effective means for obeying God's holy law, and when with our constant and confident prayers we support believers in their efforts to be faithful to the demands of the faith and to live in accordance with the Gospel (cf. *Col* 1:9–12). Especially today, Christian moral teaching must be one of the chief areas in which we exercise our pastoral vigilance, in carrying out our *munus regale.*

115 This is the first time, in fact, that the Magisterium of the Church has set forth in detail the fundamental elements of this teaching, and presented the principles for the pastoral discernment necessary in practical and cultural situations which are complex and even crucial.

In the light of Revelation and of the Church's constant teaching, especially that of the Second Vatican Council, I have briefly recalled the eseential characteristics of freedom, as well as the fundamental values connected with the dignity of the person and the truth of his acts, so as to be able to discern in obedience to the moral law a grace and a sign of our adoption in the one Son (cf. *Eph* 1:4–6). Specifically, this Encyclical has evaluated certain trends in moral theology today. I now pass this evaluation on to you, in obedience to the word of the Lord who entrusted to Peter the task of strengthening his brethren (cf. *Lk* 22:32), in order to clarify and aid our common discernment.

Each of us knows how important is the teaching which represents the central theme of this Encyclical and which is today being restated with the authority of the Successor of Peter. Each of us can see the seriousness of what is involved, not only for individuals but also for the whole of society, with the *reaffirmation of the universality and immutability of the moral commandments*, particularly those which prohibit always and without exception intrinsically evil acts.

In acknowledging these commandments, Christian hearts and our pastoral charity listen to the call of the One who "first loved us" (*1 Jn* 4:19). God asks us to be holy as he is holy (cf. *Lev* 19:2), to be—in Christ—perfect as he is perfect (cf. *Mt* 5:48). The unwavering demands of that commandment are based upon God's infinitely merciful love (cf. *Lk* 6:36), and the purpose of that commandment is to lead us, by the grace of Christ, on the path of that fullness of life proper to the children of God.

116. We have the duty, as Bishops, to *be vigilant that the word of God is faithfully taught*. My Brothers in the Episcopate, it is part of our pastoral ministry to see to it that this moral teaching is faithfully handed down and to have recourse to appropriate measures to ensure that the faithful are guarded from every doctrine and theory contrary to it. In carrying out this task we are all assisted by theologians; even so, theological opinions constitute neither the rule nor the norm of our teaching. Its authority is derived, by the assistance of the Holy Spirit and in communion *cum Petro et sub Petro*, from our fidelity to the Catholic faith which comes from the Apostles. As Bishops, we have the grave obligation to be *personally* vigilant that the "sound doctrine" (*1 Tim* 1:10) of faith and morals is taught in our Dioceses.

A particular responsibility is incumbent upon Bishops with regard to *Catholic institutions*. Whether these are agencies for the pastoral care of the family or for social work, or institutions dedicated to teaching or health care, Bishops can canonically erect and recognize these structures and delegate certain responsibilities to them. Nevertheless, Bishops are never relieved of their own personal obligations. It falls to them, in communion with the Holy See, both to grant the title "Catholic" to Church-related schools,[179] universities,[180] health-care facilities and counselling services, and, in cases of a serious failure to live up to that title, to take it away.

117. In the heart of every Christian, in the inmost depths of each person, there is always an echo of the question which the young man in the Gospel once asked Jesus: "Teacher, what good must I do to have eternal life?" (*Mt* 19:16). Everyone, however, needs to address this question to the "Good Teacher", since he is the only one who can answer in the fullness of truth, in all situations, in the most varied of

---

[179] Cf. *Code of Canon Law*, Canon 803, 3.
[180] Cf. *Code of Canon Law*, Canon 808.

circumstances. And when Christians ask him the question which rises from their conscience, the Lord replies in the words of the New Covenant which have been entrusted to his Church. As the Apostle Paul said of himself, we have been sent "to preach the Gospel, and not with eloquent wisdom, lest the Cross of Christ be emptied of its power" (*1 Cor* 1:17). The Church's answer to man's question contains the wisdom and power of Christ Crucified, the Truth which gives of itself.

When people ask the Church the questions raised by their consciences, when the faithful in the Church turn to their Bishops and Pastors, *the Church's reply contains the voice of Jesus Christ, the voice of the truth about good and evil.* In the words spoken by the Church there resounds, in people's inmost being, the voice of God who "alone is good" (cf. *Mt* 19:17), who alone "is love" (*1 Jn* 4:8, 16).

Through the *anointing of the Spirit* this gentle but challenging word becomes light and life for man. Again the Apostle Paul invites us to have confidence, because "our competence is from God, who has made us competent to be ministers of a new covenant, not in a written code but in the Spirit . . . The Lord is the Spirit, and where the Spirit of the Lord is, there is freedom. And all of us, wth unveiled faces, reflecting the glory of the Lord, are being changed into his likeness from one degree of glory to another; for this comes from the Lord, the Spirit" (*2 Cor* 3:5–6, 17–18).

CONCLUSION

Mary, Mother of Mercy

118.   At the end of these considerations, let us entrust ourselves, the sufferings and the joys of our life, the moral life of believers and people of good will, and the research of moralists, to Mary, Mother of God and Mother of Mercy.

Mary is Mother of Mercy because her Son, Jesus Christ, was sent by the Father as the revelation of God's mercy (cf. *Jn* 3:16–18). Christ came not to condemn but to forgive, to show mercy (cf. *Mt* 9:13). And the greatest mercy of all is found in his being in our midst and calling us to meet him and to confess, with Peter, that he is "the Son of the living God" (*Mt* 16:16). No human sin can erase the mercy of God, or prevent him from unleashing all his triumphant power, if we only call upon him. Indeed, sin itself makes even more radiant the love of the Father who, in order to ransom a slave, sacrificed his Son:[181] his mercy towards us is Redemption. This mercy reaches its fullness in the gift of the Spirit who bestows new life and demands that it be lived. No matter how many and great the obstacles put in his way by human frailty and sin, the Spirit, who renews the face of the earth (cf. *Ps* 104:30), makes possible the miracle of the perfect accomplishment of the good. This renewal, which gives the ability to do what is good, noble, beautiful, pleasing to God and in conformity with his will, is in some way the flowering of the gift of mercy, which offers liberation from the slavery of evil and gives the strength to sin no more. Through the gift of new life, Jesus makes us sharers in his love and leads us to the Father in the Spirit.

119.   Such is the consoling certainty of Christian faith, the source of its profound humanity and *extraordinary simplicity*. At times, in the discussions about new and complex moral problems, it can seem that Christian morality is in itself too demanding, difficult to understand and almost impossible to practise. This is untrue, since Christian morality consists, in the simplicity of the Gospel, in *following Jesus Christ*, in abandoning oneself to him, in letting oneself be transformed by his grace and renewed by his mercy, gifts which come to us in the living communion of his Church. Saint Augustine reminds us that "he who

---

[181] "O inaestimabilis dilectio caritatis: ut servum redimeres, Filium tradidisti!": *Missale Romanum, In Resurrectione Domini, Praeconium Paschale.*

would live has a place to live, and has everything needed to live. Let him draw near, let him believe, let him become part of the body, that he may have life. Let him not shrink from the unity of the members".[182] By the light of the Holy Spirit, the living essence of Christian morality can be understood by everyone, even the least learned, but particularly those who are able to preserve an "undivided heart" (Ps 86:11). On the other hand, this evangelical simplicity does not exempt one from facing reality in its complexity; rather it can lead to a more genuine understanding of reality, inasmuch as following Christ will gradually bring out the distinctive character of authentic Christian morality, while providing the vital energy needed to carry it out. It is the task of the Church's Magisterium to see that the dynamic process of following Christ develops in an organic manner, without the falsification or obscuring of its moral demands, with all their consequences. The one who loves Christ keeps his commandments (cf. Jn 14:15).

120.   Mary is also Mother of Mercy because it is to her that Jesus entrusts his Church and all humanity. At the foot of the Cross, when she accepts John as her son, when she asks, together with Christ, forgiveness from the Father for those who do not know what they do (cf. Lk 23:34), Mary experiences, in perfect docility to the Spirit, the richness and the universality of God's love, which opens her heart and enables it to embrace the entire human race. Thus Mary becomes Mother of each and every one of us, the Mother who obtains for us divine mercy.

Mary is the radiant sign and inviting model of the moral life. As Saint Ambrose put it, "The life of this one person can serve as a model for everyone",[183] and while speaking specifically to virgins but within a context open to all, he affirmed: "The first stimulus to learning is the nobility of the teacher. Who can be more noble than the Mother of God? Who can be more glorious than the one chosen by Glory Itself?"[184] Mary lived and exercised her freedom precisely by giving herself to God and accepting God's gift within herself. Until the time of his birth, she sheltered in her womb the Son of God who became man; she raised him and enabled him to grow, and she accompanied him in that supreme act of freedom which is the complete sacrifice of his own life. By the gift of herself, Mary entered fully into the plan of God who gives himself to the world. By accepting and pondering in her heart events which she did not always understand (cf. Lk 2:19), she became the model of all those who hear the word of God and keep it (cf. Lk 11:28), and merited the title of

---

[182] In Iohannis Evangelium Tractatus, 26, 13: CCL, 36, 266.
[183] De Virginibus, Bk. II, Chap. II, 15: PL 16, 222.
[184] Ibid., Bk. II, Chap. II, 7: PL 16, 220.

"Seat of Wisdom". This Wisdom is Jesus Christ himself, the Eternal Word of God, who prefectly reveals and accomplishes the will of the Father (cf. *Heb* 10:5–10). Mary invites everyone to accept this Wisdom. To us too she addresses the command she gave to the servants at Cana in Galilee during the marriage feast: "Do whatever he tells you" (*Jn* 2:5).

Mary shares our human condition, but in complete openness to the grace of God. Not having known sin, she is able to have compassion on every kind of weakness. She understands sinful man and loves him with a Mother's love. Precisely for this reason she is on the side of truth and shares the Church's burden in recalling always and to everyone the demands of morality. Nor does she permit sinful man to be deceived by those who claim to love him by justifying his sin, for she knows that the sacrifice of Christ her Son would thus be emptied of its power. No absolution offered by beguiling doctrines, even in the areas of philosophy and theology, can make man truly happy: only the Cross and the glory of the Risen Christ can grant peace to his conscience and salvation to his life.

O Mary,
Mother of Mercy,
watch over all people,
that the Cross of Christ
may not be emptied of its power,
that man may not stray
from the path of the good
or become blind to sin,
but may put his hope ever more fully in God
who is "rich in mercy" (*Eph* 2:4).
May he carry out the good works prepared
by God beforehand (cf. *Eph* 2:10)
and so live completely
"for the praise of his glory" (*Eph* 1:12).

Given in Rome, at Saint Peter's, on 6 August, Feast of the Transfiguration of the Lord, in the year 1993, the fifteenth of my Pontificate.

Joannes Paulus II